It's My Party Too

It's My Party Too

*The Battle for
the Heart of the GOP
and the Future of America*

Christine Todd Whitman

THE PENGUIN PRESS
New York
2005

THE PENGUIN PRESS
Published by the Penguin Group
Penguin Group (USA) Inc., 375 Hudson Street, New York, New York 10014, U.S.A. •
Penguin Group (Canada), 10 Alcorn Avenue, Toronto, Ontario, Canada M4V 3B2 (a division
of Pearson Penguin Canada Inc.) • Penguin Books Ltd, 80 Strand, London WC2R 0RL,
England • Penguin Ireland, 25 St. Stephen's Green, Dublin 2, Ireland (a division of Penguin
Books Ltd) • Penguin Books Australia Ltd, 250 Camberwell Road, Camberwell, Victoria 3124,
Australia (a division of Pearson Australia Group Pty Ltd) • Penguin Books India Pvt Ltd,
11 Community Centre, Panchsheel Park, New Delhi - 110 017, India • Penguin Group (NZ),
Cnr Airborne and Rosedale Roads, Albany, Auckland 1310, New Zealand (a division of Pearson
New Zealand Ltd) • Penguin Books (South Africa) (Pty) Ltd, 24 Sturdee Avenue, Rosebank,
Johannesburg 2196, South Africa • Penguin Books Ltd, Registered Offices:
80 Strand, London WC2R 0RL, England

First published in 2005 by The Penguin Press,
a member of Penguin Group (USA) Inc.

Copyright © Christine Todd Whitman, 2005
All rights reserved

CIP data available

ISBN 1-59420-040-8

This book is printed on acid-free paper. ∞

Printed in the United States of America
1   3   5   7   9   10   8   6   4   2

Designed by Claire Vaccaro

This book is dedicated to the two people who started me on my journey, my parents, and to the one man who made it possible for me to succeed, my husband, John. Our children, Kate and Taylor, have been gracious and supportive no matter what was thrown at them and my sister, Kate, and brothers John and Dan tried valiantly to keep me in line. I love you all.

Contents

ONE   Does the Right Make Might?   1

TWO   Whatever Happened to the Big Umbrella?   29

THREE   The Party Within the Party   71

FOUR   Reclaiming Lincoln's Legacy   101

FIVE   This Land Is Our Land   143

SIX   A Woman in the Party   197

SEVEN   A Time for Radical Moderates   227

Acknowledgments   245

CHAPTER ONE

Does the Right Make Might?

So today I want to speak to every person who voted for my opponent.
To make this nation stronger and better, I will need your support, and
I will work to earn it. I will do all I can to deserve your trust.

PRESIDENT GEORGE W. BUSH, NOVEMBER 3, 2004

We stand at a historic juncture in American politics, a critical crossroads for both the Republican Party and for the nation. The choice to be made is momentous. Will the GOP interpret the president's reelection victory as a mandate, even a requirement, to continue to cater to the demands of the far right on a series of key wedge issues? If so, the party will further fuel the fires of overheated polarization by pushing positions that alienate tens of millions of Americans. The recent demand for a total ban on all embryonic stem cell research and the call for amending the Constitution to prohibit gay marriage—only the second time in history an amendment would restrict individual freedom—are just two examples of policies that will jeopardize the long-term viability of the party's margin of victory. Or, at this critical crossroads, will the party decide to broaden its base into a stronger, long-lasting majority by returning to a focus on the core Republican values? Those core values—smaller government, fiscal responsibility, and strong security—unite conservatives and moderates, even moderates in the Democratic Party, as Ronald Reagan proved. If the GOP musters the will to move forward in that more expansive way, it cannot only consolidate its hold on power, but also heal the wounds of extreme polarization and make great strides in facing the many challenges ahead.

The party must remember that while winning elections is surely important, it is every bit as important to win them in ways that allow you to govern all the people once the ballots are counted. The president was clear in his victory speech that he wants "the broad support of Americans," and he pledged that he would "work to earn it" from those who opposed him. But the rhetoric from the leadership of the far-right faction, even today, shows no indication of willingness to reach out—either to those within the party or those outside it—on anything other than their terms.

Just hours after the president declared victory, one longtime conservative activist, Richard Viguerie, wrote, "Now comes the revolution. . . . Make no mistake—conservative Christians and 'values voters' won this election for George W. Bush and Republicans in Congress. It's crucial that the Republican leadership not forget this—as much as some will try." James Dobson, the head of the conservative group Focus on the Family, asserted that President Bush must now move to pass a constitutional amendment regulating marriage, to overturn *Roe v. Wade,* and also to prohibit all embryonic stem cell research. "I believe that the Bush administration now needs to be more aggressive in pursuing these values," he said, "and if they don't do it I believe they will pay a price in four years." Christian conservative organizer Phil Burress boldly proclaimed, "The president rode our coattails," while another, Austin Ruse, said that his pro-life group has essentially "earned" the right to name the next chief justice of the Supreme Court.

These groups—headed by people I call social fundamentalists, whose sole mission is to advance their narrow ideological agenda—argue that they tipped the balance in the election and that the party can't win elections without them. As the Reverend Jerry Falwell said just weeks before the election, "The Republican Party does not have the head count to elect a president without the support of religious conservatives. I tell my Republican friends who are always talking about the 'big tent,' I say make it as big as you want to but if the candidate running for president is not pro-life, pro-family, you're not going to win."

Yes, it's true that President Bush won more votes in 2004 than any other president, and that evangelical voters contributed to that victory. A less publicized fact is that the president's 3-percentage-point popular vote margin was the smallest margin of any incumbent president ever to win reelection. Bill Clinton won his reelection battle by more than 8 points, Ronald Reagan won his by 18 points, and Richard Nixon was reelected by 23 points. Even Harry Truman, whom everyone had written off by the time the polls closed on Election Day 1948, ended up beating his opponent by nearly 5 points.

Even in the 2004 presidential election, of the fifty-nine million people who cast their ballots for President Bush, only twenty million identified moral values as their most important issue. That's not even a majority of the votes the president received—it's only a third. Given those numbers, and the fact that evangelicals represented the same proportion of voters in 2004 as they did in 2000, the party has to ask itself if the evangelicals' claim for making the president's victory possible aren't possibly overblown. We must also consider whether or not a little more outreach to moderates might not have brought the party an even greater victory. After all, while moderate voters ranked the economy and the war on terror as higher priorities, they too are concerned about America's moral values.

In New Jersey, where I was the cochair of the reelection campaign, President Bush cut the Democrats' margin of victory in 2000 by more than half. He achieved similar inroads in such blue states as Washington and Hawaii. These numbers indicate that states such as these might have been winnable if the party had worked harder at attracting moderates. If they had, he might now have a much stronger mandate.

The numbers show that while the president certainly did energize his political base, the red state/blue state map changed barely at all—suggesting that he had missed an opportunity to significantly broaden his support in the most populous areas of the country. The Karl Rove strategy to focus so rigorously on the narrow conservative base won the day, but we must ask at what price to governing and at what risk to the future of the party. When fully a quarter of the public told the Gallup Poll immediately after the election that they were *afraid* of a second Bush term, we have to be concerned.

One of the most important truths in the 2004 campaign—one that has been overlooked by the mainstream media for years—is that in the post–Clinton era, the Democratic Party largely abandoned the center it occupied for a brief time in the 1990s. That leftward shift played right into Rove's hands. Many Americans came to believe that the Democrat leadership simply didn't care about the traditional American values of integrity, fidelity, self-discipline, and faith. There's no doubt that most Americans found the overall Republican message more in tune with their values. Nevertheless, many in the huge center of the American electorate are also put off by the more extreme positions of the far-right groups.

A clear and present danger Republicans face today is that the party will now move so far to the right that it ends up alienating centrist voters and marginalizing itself. It's naïve, after all, to presume that the Democrats won't learn from their mistakes and move closer to the center for the next round. The president was right when he said in his victory statement "when we come together and work together, there is no limit to the greatness of America." Unfortunately, after this most recent campaign, realizing that dream will be extremely difficult. By focusing so much on the demands of the social fundamentalists and their allies on the far right during the first term, the White House created a high level of expectations in that wing of the party that will be hard to resist.

In moving forward, it is important to remember that the president didn't win reelection with the social fundamentalists alone. The special importance of the moderates to the president's re-election was proven time and again during the campaign. The social fundamentalists forget that in the closing days of the 2004 campaign, when President Bush was fighting hard to secure a victory in Ohio, he didn't ask Jerry Falwell, or Pat Robertson, or James Dobson to campaign with him; he brought Arnold Schwarzenegger and Rudy Giuliani along, and their efforts also helped him win.

Then there is the lesson of the Republican National Convention. The Bush team spent more than two hundred million dollars in the months running up to the 2004 Republican National Convention, seeking both to shore up the president's political base and break the seemingly unbreakable deadlock in the polls between the president and Senator Kerry. For months, virtually every poll in America showed the president's support stuck somewhere in the mid-40s. The race was considered a dead heat, with neither candidate's gaining any ground on his own or taking any away from his opponent. Senator Kerry was unable to get any bounce from his convention in Boston; for the first time since 1972, a party convention failed to give its candidate a positive bump in the polls. That seemed to reinforce the view that the electorate was split right down the middle, with very little opportunity for either candidate to break the deadlock.

By early July, however, the Bush campaign decided it needed to make a course correction. When the prime-time speaking schedule for the Republican National Convention in New York was announced, the program featured one prominent moderate Republican after another: Rudolph Giuliani, John McCain, Arnold Schwarzenegger, George Pataki.

The social fundamentalist leadership was not pleased. One veteran Christian conservative operative wrote in his regular e-mail newsletter, "I hate to say it, but the conservatives, for the most part, are not excited about re-electing the president. If the president is embarrassed to be seen with conservatives at the convention, maybe conservatives will be embarrassed to be seen with the president on Election Day." The Washington editor of the *National Review*, Kate O'Beirne, wrote, "If the lineup is intended to make an overwhelmingly conservative party attractive to swing voters, it does so by pretending to be something it's not."

O'Beirne, however, could not have been more wrong. Those speakers at the convention, far from representing something the party is not, are, in fact, among the most popular politicians in the country. By the time the convention was over, America had seen a different face of the GOP, and it apparently liked what it saw. President Bush received an 11-point bounce, giving him his first real lead in the polls all year. It wasn't until the GOP showcased its moderate side—emphasizing its bedrock principles—that the people responded positively in the polls.

The social conservatives and their allies will probably never acknowledge the impact those four days of the convention had on voters' perceptions of the president and the party. The day after the convention closed, Rush Limbaugh argued in the *Wall Street Journal* that because Schwarzenegger, Giuliani, and McCain hadn't talked about abortion or gay marriage, they were hiding their moderate views from the American people—as if the people watching didn't know that these leaders were moderates. Limbaugh missed the point. The moderates who spoke at the convention succeeded in driving up support for the president precisely because they focused on the core issues that unite all Republicans: less government, lower taxes, and strong national security. Clearly many voters who were not sure prior to the convention about President Bush and the Republicans were convinced by what they heard from the convention that the party was not only willing to make room for moderate voices; it was willing to embrace them.

I liked what Peggy Noonan, the most articulate voice of the conservatives in the Republican Party, had to say about Schwarzenegger's speech, in which he clearly and unambiguously articulated the core principles of the Republican Party when he said: "If you believe that government should be accountable to the people, not the people to the government . . . if you believe a person should be treated as an individual, not as a member of an interest group . . . if you believe your family knows how to spend your money better than the government does . . . then you are a Republican." As Noonan said, "I think Arnold's speech was historic—redefining Republicanism in a way that all of us on the floor could agree with, and people at home could think about and ponder." My sentiments exactly.

From where I sat, the 2004 convention was the best since 1988. For the first time in sixteen years, I felt at home among, not estranged from, my fellow Republicans from all over the country and all up and down the political spectrum. There was far less anger and far more unity than I had seen or experienced in years. I had a palpable sense that perhaps the party was beginning to regain its moorings, starting to recognize the need to gather all those who share a firm commitment to traditional Republican principles under the big umbrella my father told me about almost fifty years ago. When a Republican national convention is brought to its feet by an Austrian immigrant, former bodybuilder, and one-time action movie star who just happens to also be the pro-choice, pro-environment, anti-gay–marriage amendment Republican governor of the largest state in America, that's a sign that things could change. It also suggests how much more decisive a victory the president could have achieved if he had campaigned on the values and messages of those moderates.

The fact is that moderate Republican candidates have won elections in America's largest and third largest states and its largest city, California, New York, and New Your City—places, incidentally, that Republican presidential candidates haven't carried in years. Between them, Schwarzenegger and Pataki represent nearly one of every five Americans. Showcasing them and their brand of moderate Republicanism isn't pretending to be something the party isn't. It's showcasing a vital, and substantial, element of the party without which Republicans would quickly become a marginalized force in American politics. The popularity of these moderate leaders points the way to what more the party can become if it will only commit to making room—real room—in the leadership for moderates.

But will the party make the right choice? Because the president cannot run again—and Vice President Cheney will not—the party has no heir (or heiress) apparent for the 2008 presidential election. Yet if the social fundamentalists prevail, Republicans like Rudy Giuliani, Tom Ridge, and Colin Powell—all outstanding leaders with broad national appeal—won't even have a chance of winning the party's nomination because of their pro-choice principles. The GOP cannot afford to eliminate its most popular potential candidates from contention because they don't pass the favorite litmus test of the far right.

The problem, of course, with the party's making a course correction toward moderation is that the far-right groups, which have so powerfully consolidated their power within the party, have no interest in doing so. Not only do they have no interest in moving the party closer to the center, but they are outright hostile toward the moderate ranks. More than ever before in modern times, the Republican Party at the national level is allowing itself to be dictated to by a coalition of these small but fervid groups that have claimed the mantle of conservatism, and the leadership of these groups shows no inclination to seek bipartisan consensus on anything. The Democrats are facing the same challenge from union leadership and trial lawyers. My concern, however, is with Republicans.

I remember a group of western Republican congressmen telling me early in my tenure at the Environmental Protection Agency that if they ever read a favorable editorial in the *New York Times* about the Bush administration's environmental policy, "we might as well still have a Democrat president." What the leaders of this coalition forget is that not every question of governing hinges on a question of rigid principle, and on most questions there is ample room to find productive middle ground. Indeed, from my experience in politics, on most questions the middle ground is the only productive ground.

The leaders of these groups seek to impose rigid litmus tests on Republican candidates and appear determined to drive out of the party anyone who doesn't subscribe to their beliefs in their entirety. Organizations like the Club for Growth see no inconsistency in their pursuit of electing a Republican majority in Congress and their efforts to defeat Republican incumbents in divisive and costly primaries. Another influential group is

Americans for Tax Reform, whose idea of politically sophisticated thinking is to "oppose all tax increases as a matter of principle" and to refuse to support any Republican candidate who doesn't sign the group's no-tax pledge. These and other social fundamentalist groups share an apparent desire to purge the party of "nonbelievers." They would dispute my assertion that there's room in the party for all those who share basic Republican principles but might disagree on particular issues (such as whether there might, at some point, actually be the need for a tax increase of some sort, perhaps like the one Ronald Reagan signed into law in 1986). As far as they're concerned, the Republican Party isn't my party too; it's their party period.

They call us moderates RINOs—Republicans in Name Only. But they fail to acknowledge that without RINOs like Olympia Snowe and Susan Collins of Maine, Arlen Specter of Pennsylvania, Nancy Johnson of Connecticut, Rodney Frelinghuysen of New Jersey, Jerry Lewis of California, Jim McCrery of Louisiana, Jim Leach of Iowa, and many others the GOP would never have won the majority in Congress in 1994 and still wouldn't have it today. The social fundamentalists see RINOs as apostates who are not true to the Republican cause. But the fact is that the RINOs have also not turned away from the party, much as some people—both Democrats and Republicans—might wish they would. On the contrary, they strongly supported President Bush's reelection.

Moderates have an indispensable role to play: We must bring the Republican Party, and American politics generally, back toward the productive center. But that won't happen easily. It is time for Republican moderates to assert forcefully and plainly that this is our party too, that we not only have a place, but a

:e—and not just a voice, but a vision—a vision that is true to tne historic principles of our party and our nation, not one tied to an extremist agenda.

If we believe the government has a responsibility to be prudent in its use of taxpayer dollars and not to run up huge deficits that will ultimately tax our children and grandchildren, we must push for fiscal responsibility and should seek to couple tax cuts with restraint on spending.

It we believe that every woman has the right to make choices about her pregnancy, without interference from the government, we must not support the appointment of judges who vow to overturn *Roe v. Wade*.

If we believe that the Constitution protects individual freedom from an intrusive central government, then we must oppose a constitutional amendment to regulate or define marriage, and leave the matter where it belongs—with the states.

If we believe that protecting the environment is essential and is a public responsibility and a Republican issue, we must insist on advancing a pro-active agenda that actually results in cleaner air, purer water, and better-protected land.

If we believe the United States has a vital role to play as the world's only superpower in leading the world both with strength and wisdom, then we must push for a foreign policy premised on the understanding that the rest of the world matters to us. We must advocate against becoming ensnared in nation-building enterprises and push for policies that engage us with the world community and show, in the words of the Declaration of Independence, "a decent respect to the opinions of mankind."

If moderates don't rally around the core principles that have long defined Republicanism, the extreme right will run away with the party. Preventing that troubling fate will take the emergence of "radical moderates."

The moderates in the Republican Party today face a momentous choice. We can decide to continue to "go along to get along," to yield when push comes to shove to preserve the unity of the party and our place in it. Or we can elect to draw a line in the sand, to decide that the future of Republicanism is too important to allow those who seek to purge the party of anyone who is "ideologically impure" to take over. This is, as Ronald Reagan once said, a time for choosing.

The battle, of course, will not be easy, as I learned all too clearly from my time serving as head of the Environmental Protection Agency. I've been around politics long enough to know that it's not for the faint of heart. After all, I've spent most of my career in New Jersey politics, where extreme partisanship is an official state sport. Yet nothing I saw in more than fifteen years as an elected official, or in a lifetime as a participant around politics at the local, state, and national levels, prepared me for what I witnessed in Washington in early 2001.

I joined the administration cautiously optimistic that the extreme bitterness of the Florida recount—in which actual fights had broken out at one polling place—and the Supreme Court decision on the election could be put behind us. I was eager to start work at the EPA and, given the environmental improvements we'd been able to achieve in New Jersey when I was governor, I felt reasonably confident my time at the agency would be productive. President Bush had pledged to bring a spirit of bipartisanship to his administration, and hard as it is to recall now, in those first days there was at least one glimmer of hope. The Senate was divided 50–50 between the parties for the first time in history. Yet after just two weeks of negotiation in the first week of January 2001, the Republican and Democratic leaders of the Senate, Trent Lott and Tom Daschle, reached a power-sharing agreement aimed at avoiding partisan gridlock. I thought that if Lott and Daschle, who had just traded places as Senate majority leader, could agree on how to divide power, perhaps the rest of the government really could move forward in the same manner.

After all, as governor of Texas, George W. Bush had developed a reputation for effectively reaching across party lines to find common ground. He had forged such a close working relationship with the top-ranking Democrat in Texas that the then lieutenant governor, Bob Bullock, supported Bush for reelection as governor in 1998, even though Bullock was a close friend of Bush's Democratic opponent, Garry Mauro. Bullock was even godfather to one of Mauro's daughters. Given that impressive Texas track record, I sincerely believed that President Bush hoped to be able to replicate that success in Washington.

I'm sometimes asked these days why I took the EPA position—didn't I realize I'd walked into a no-win situation? Hard as it is to believe now, the fact is that heading into the inauguration, many of us accepting appointments believed we had the opportunity to work with Democrats to create an effective administration that could unite rather than divide the country. Unfortunately, the Democrats showed only a limited interest in working cooperatively.

Before accepting the position at EPA, I met with the president-elect, the vice president-elect, and a few members of the new senior White House staff, including Andy Card and Karl Rove, at the transition headquarters in a hotel suite in Washington. I had known George W. Bush and Dick Cheney for a long time, so the meeting itself was comfortable and straightforward.

I first met President Bush when he was elected governor of Texas in 1994. Through the National Governors Association, I had had numerous opportunities to see him in action. We had also served as cochairs of the 1996 Republican National Convention in San Diego. He and I and our staffs had shared the same trailer behind the platform, so we got the chance to know each other a little better during the convention's four days. Although nothing was said explicitly, I got the impression Governor Bush was definitely eyeing the presidency himself. Members of my staff said they came away with the same impression from their interactions with his staff.

Dick Cheney and I went way back—back to my first job in Washington in 1969, when he was a close colleague of my boss, Don Rumsfeld, at the Office of Equal Opportunity and I was an executive assistant. I have always found Dick to be intelligent, insightful, and understated. He did far more listening than talking, which is a rare trait in Washington. Even at the age of thirty, he seemed like an elder statesman. He never impressed me as a conservative ideologue; over the years, I always thought his wife, Lynne, a distinguished scholar in her own right, was the more conservative. When Dick called to offer me the job at EPA, he did so in his usual cordial, straightforward, businesslike fashion. I was struck at the time by how far we both had come—from my days at a small government agency, which President Nixon had hoped to abolish, to his becoming vice president-elect and calling to offer me a job in the new president's cabinet.

The icebreaker at that meeting at transition headquarters was the dog the president-elect had recently purchased from me as a present for the first lady. Just days before the election, during a campaign stop in New Jersey as he lamented not having a birthday present for Laura, I told the soon-to-be president-elect about my dog's new puppies, and he immediately asked me about getting one for Mrs. Bush. Although I offered to give the puppy to the Bushes, he insisted on paying for him—he didn't want any appearance of impropriety (although I can't imagine that anyone would think he traded the job of EPA administrator for a dog). The puppy, a cute Scottish terrier the Bushes named Barney, had been delivered to the president-elect's suite earlier that day, and he was making himself right at home. Although Dick Cheney didn't seem to care much for the new dog—especially after Barney christened the carpet in all the excitement—the Bushes certainly did, as the many photo ops that Barney has been a part of over the years have shown. In fact, in keeping with what was becoming an election-year tradition, two weeks before the election in 2004, we found another New Jersey scottie puppy for the president to give the first lady.

I came away from our meeting optimistic that the president-elect and I were in accord when it came to national environmental policy. As governors, we had each butted up against environmental regulations written in Washington that didn't work well in our own states. We also agreed that the states are often far ahead of Washington in developing innovative solutions to environmental challenges. We both believed that the time had come to strike a balance, that environmental policy had become too heavily weighted toward the "command and control" mode of operation—with everything being directed from Washington, micromanaged to an unreasonable and unproductive degree.

I also had no doubt that President Bush wanted a strong environmental record to be part of both his agenda and his legacy. That belief was reinforced when Karl Rove told me after that meeting that I would be one of just three cabinet officers who would help determine whether the president would be reelected. At the time, I took Rove to mean that the work I would do in building a strong record on the environment would help the president build on his base by attracting moderate swing voters. As it turned out, I don't seem to have understood Karl correctly.

My confirmation hearing, though nerve-racking, was similarly uneventful. I benefited, in part, from the Democrats' decision to make John Ashcroft the focus of their wrath in the first round of confirmation battles. Because I had a strong record on environmental issues as governor of New Jersey, I expected to have solid support, and I believed that I truly had a chance to build a consensus on how to move forward to achieve the next generation of environmental progress. I knew there would be partisan wrangling over exactly how to proceed. My experience in New Jersey had taught me plenty about just how bitterly partisan the battle over environmental policy has become. I nonetheless thought that we had an opportunity really to accomplish something: to leave America's air cleaner, its water purer, and its land better protected than we had found it. That belief was short-lived.

Once I arrived in Washington, it became abundantly clear that the consequences of the Florida recount were far more traumatic, and ran far deeper, than I had expected. The Democrats were bitter, both from the Clinton impeachment and the recount. Although the courtesy meetings with various senators prior to my confirmation hearings were cordial, it was nevertheless obvious that lines already were being drawn. Members of the Senate Committee on Environment and Public Works, which had primary jurisdiction over the EPA, made sure I knew they would be watching very closely for any missteps. One leading Democrat told me point-blank that although he had no problem with me, he didn't trust the president. His meaning was clear: Don't expect a honeymoon.

As for the Republicans, too many in my own party so relished the victories we had won—which put the party in control of the White House and both houses of Congress for the first time in almost fifty years—that they saw little reason to reach out to build a bipartisan consensus on much of anything. Their hubris was inflated when word came out, right after President Clinton left Washington, that he had issued a last-minute flurry of 140 pardons, including several to people closely connected to the Democratic Party and its fund-raising operations. Many Republicans thought that with all the resulting bad press, Bill Clinton's legacy would continue to be an albatross around the Democrats' necks, and Republicans would have that weakness to exploit as the Bush administration took charge. That attitude contributed its fair share to the overheated partisanship that subsequently gripped not only Washington, but also the whole country.

As I witnessed—and experienced—the escalating partisan warfare firsthand in Washington, I asked myself, Where has the process broken down? When had the Senate been transformed from the world's greatest deliberative body into an arena for childish name calling? When had House members morphed from generally respectful colleagues—people who knew how to conduct passionate debates during the day while still maintaining the basic civility to meet one another for friendly dinners at night—into such close-minded and defiant adversaries that they barely spoke to one another in the halls? Why was this same bitterness infecting state houses around the country, and what does it mean for our country and its future?

As we have seen in recent years, most acutely during the 2004 campaign, the harsh tenor of our politics today is infecting the entire body politic, making it increasingly difficult to hold rational discussions about the most important issues facing the country. We spend more time trying to demonize our opponents than we do trying to discuss issues. The challenges we face are simply too important to allow this to continue.

Ever since our founding, Americans have believed that every person has the unlimited possibility to achieve success, based on their abilities and desires. Implicit in that approach is the recognition that not everyone will take the same path, want the same thing, or find themselves in the same place at any point in time. A political party that does not recognize this fundamental precept of American life will not only overlook the wonderful strength that our diversity has long brought us, but will also end up being rejected by the very people it seeks to attract.

These various far-right constituencies of the GOP are, in reality, nothing more than narrow interest groups, and they have not only been demanding that the party leadership kowtow to them; they have actually been seeking to take over the broader party and push the moderates out. In recent years, moderate Republicans who have strayed from this hard-line orthodoxy have been targeted by activists seeking to purge them from the party using primary ballots instead of bullets. The 2004 Pennsylvania Republican primary for the Senate perfectly illustrates the intensity of their vitriol and the counterproductiveness of their zealotry.

Arlen Specter, a four-team moderate Republican senator in a swing state, was challenged in the primary by Patrick Toomey, an archconservative Republican congressman who could be a poster child for the ideological zealots who are trying to exclude from the party those who don't share their views. Toomey justified his challenge by saying, "The problem we've got is a handful of Republican senators who never really bought into the idea of the Republican Party in the first place. I represent the Republican wing of the Republican Party." As one of Toomey's most prominent supporters put it, "If we beat Specter, we won't have any trouble with wayward Republicans anymore." Specter won (with the support of President Bush and his fellow Pennsylvania senator, Rick Santorum, himself a much more conservative Republican than Specter), but as far as the ideological zealots were concerned, their candidate's defeat still served an important purpose. Stephen Moore, the head of the Club for Growth and a significant supporter of Toomey, claimed that the challenge to Specter also "serve[d] notice to Chafee, Snowe, Voinovich [all moderate Republican senators] and others who have been problem children that they will be next." Specter, incidentally, went on to win reelection by 700,000 votes, even as the president was losing Pennsylvania by 100,000.

Specter was hardly alone. Other congressional moderates have had to weather similar assaults, including a longtime friend of mine, former representative Marge Roukema. New Jersey's only woman in Congress for almost twenty years, Marge twice fought off well-financed far-right challenges, only to eventually decide to retire rather than battle in a primary for a third time. Last year, as the *Washington Post* reported, "In New York state alone, Amo Houghton and Jack Quinn, two House members representing the face of Republican moderation, have announced their retirements." As Houghton said after making known his plans, "I would like to make sure the Republican Party is centered. We veered too much to the right." Unfortunately, many Republican moderates have grown weary of the battle and are retreating to the sidelines. We need them to stay engaged.

For a long time now, we moderates have given too much ground to those whose agenda is not to build the party but rather to advance their own narrow ideology. We know that good policy makes for good politics, but we have been too willing to appease those on the extreme, even as they pursue an agenda that's ultimately neither good policy nor good politics. It's time for moderates to accommodate less and demand more.

Perhaps the most troubling aspect of the social fundamentalists' consolidation of power is the increased movement toward restricting choices. Like fundamentalist movements around the world, the concept of choice—of there being a legitimate range of options and outcomes—is anathema to extreme social fundamentalists.

The party leadership's insistence on meeting the demands of the extreme social fundamentalists has overshadowed its broader commitment to cutting taxes, containing the growth of government, reducing welfare, fighting crime, and helping the private sector create jobs. Those are the issues I've focused on as a Republican. During the seven years I was governor of New Jersey we achieved a strong record of Republican success: Taxes were cut more than fifty times, saving the taxpayers more than fifteen billion dollars; the growth of government spending was held to its lowest average in forty years, less than the rate of inflation; the welfare rolls were cut in half; crime was reduced to a thirty-year low; and unemployment was reduced by half, with more people working than ever in the history of the state. That's a good conservative record. Yet I took a great deal of heat from ideological extremists when I was governor because I support a woman's right to choose.

In 1997, when I ran for reelection, a group of lawmakers within my own party who disagreed with me on choice refused to support me, even going so far as to encourage someone named Murray Sabrin, a college teacher with no political experience or credentials, to run against me as a Libertarian in the general election. In doing so, they nearly turned over the governor's office to my Democratic opponent. If I had received even half of the 114,000 votes Sabrin garnered in that election, I would have won by about 100,000 votes in a state that had elected only one other Republican to statewide office in the previous twenty-five years. What's more, the closeness of that election set the stage for Democrat Jim McGreevey's gubernatorial victory in 2001 and a

Democratic sweep of both houses of the legislature in 2003. That's no way for Republicans to consolidate a majority or to ensure political relevancy. Unfortunately, the new breed of Republican ideological extremists seems to forget that in order to be able to implement its party agenda, the first goal of any political party is to win elections. Too many of them would rather be "right" than be in power.

There's no doubt party leadership has allowed a few hot-button issues—on which this "new conservative coalition" has taken hard-line positions—to steer it off course, and the extremism on those issues has helped drive the overheated polarization of the American public. On the social issues, on race, and on the environment, extremists within the Republican Party are pushing views that are alienating many of those in the mainstream and holding the party back from attaining true majority leadership in the country.

What, then, will happen to the party if this trend continues? Will more and more Americans become more and more conservative? Or will the party end up marginalizing itself? Throughout the course of America's history, whichever party most closely identifies with the mainstream of political thought—which in the United States has always run down the middle of the road— tends to have been most successful. When either party comes to be dominated by political forces that fall too much outside the mainstream of political thinking, that party becomes increasingly unable to win elections, and thus pursue its policy goals, until it rights itself and moves back to the center. That's why for most of the modern political era, the parties have sought to win elections by appealing to the broadest number of voters. Although each party has had its core constituency, moderates have usually held the key to victory.

When the Democratic Party was taken over by the far left in the late 1960s, it lost five out of the next six presidential elections. Americans didn't trust the Democrats with the White House because they didn't trust the ability of their presidential candidates to manage the extreme left-wing faction of their party and resist their influence on policy. Only when Bill Clinton was able to assure Americans that he was a "New Democrat" who would govern from the center were the Democrats able to capture the White House for two consecutive elections for the first time since 1964. Clinton was calculating about demonstrating his moderation, in part, by making some very clear moves designed to show his independence from the Democratic left wing. The most notable, perhaps, was when he repudiated an outrageous statement made by a black rapper, Sister Souljah, even while prominent black activists were defending her. Today, the Republican Party, in catering to the right wing, may well be in the process of repeating the mistake the Democrats made in the sixties with the left.

Richard Nixon's famous advice to Republicans was to run to the right in the primary and then move back to the center for the general election. This calculation worked for Republican candidates from Eisenhower through George H. W. Bush's first election, largely because they never had to go so far to the right that they couldn't come back to the center. Until the social fundamentalists cut the first President Bush adrift in his reelection campaign in 1992, Republicans had won seven of the previous ten presidential elections. (They thought he had squandered the Reagan legacy and withheld their support, helping make possible eight years of Bill Clinton. Did they really prefer that?) The record since has been somewhat more mixed.

Zell Miller, the Democratic senator from Georgia, wrote a book in 2003, *A National Party No More,* which talks about this trend in his party. Zell and I served as governors together for a time. He is one of those Democrats who think that their party has moved too far to the left, outside the mainstream of American political thought on such issues as national defense, tax policy, welfare reform, gun control, and abortion. I found his arguments resonating with me, from the other side of the aisle, and I know that many moderate Republicans, who have watched their party move rightward, feel the same sort of alienation.

During my years as governor of New Jersey and administrator of the EPA, I found myself in the middle of some of the most contentious, divisive issues in America today, such as race, abortion, and the environment. I have seen firsthand the damage that can be done in a political civil war, and the difficulties such battles pose to winning and then maintaining a political majority. I have also seen how well the party can do when moderates and conservatives work together in pursuit of the goals they share: the basic principles that make them Republicans.

Despite finding myself in the midst of such controversial issues, I navigated through them fairly successfully because, in no small measure, I was able to appeal to the moderate sensibilities of the electorate. Someone said to me recently, "Any one of several of the things you have gone through would have been enough to destroy most politicians' careers." That may or may not be true. But I do know this: At a time when our country remains evenly divided between the parties and when the parties are increasingly turning to their bases to try to win elections, an enormous number of Americans find themselves in the middle of the political spectrum and feel they have no place to go. If the Republican Party would get serious about appealing to them, it could not only build a much more impressive majority but also make substantial headway in bringing the country together again.

The past fifteen years have been a fascinating ride for me. Shortly after I was elected governor in 1993, becoming the first person in modern New Jersey political history to defeat the incumbent in a general election, I was touted as the "brightest female star within the Republican Party." More recently, one observer said of my early days at the EPA that I had "suffered the most immediate and visible loss of clout for a cabinet officer." The truth, as usual, lies somewhere in between.

There is no doubt that the moderate Republicanism I grew up with and that helped me win two statewide elections in New Jersey has been seen as being in eclipse in the national party for more than a decade. I am often asked why I am still a Republican. People who know my politics, who have seen the rightward lurch of the party and know that there are many in the GOP who have worked to exclude me wonder why I stay. I have even been approached by people who think the time has come for a third party that would unite moderates of both parties. When I get that question, I always think back to a cover story about me that ran in *The New York Times Magazine* in the spring of 1996. There was a picture of me on the cover accompanied by the headline IT'S MY PARTY TOO.

I liked that message so much that I had the cover framed

and hung it in my offices in Trenton and then in Washington. I also decided to use it as the title of this book. To moderate Republicans, that headline proclaimed our belief that there was still room for us in the party of Lincoln. Of course, the social fundamentalists in the party had one of their own verities reinforced: Only the *New York Times* would think Christie Whitman was any kind of Republican.

Yet the Republican Party is not just the party of the right wing—it *is* my party too. The basic principles that define Republicanism have not changed. We still believe in limited government, lower taxes, the power of the markets, and a strong national defense. Those basic core beliefs are shared by millions of Americans who, although they may not be comfortable with the rightward shift in the party, are not ready to give up on it. The way to change the party is from within. That is why I stay.

The people of this country deserve better from their politics and their politicians than they've been getting in recent years. It doesn't have to be this way. You can be passionate and civil, believe deeply and yet respect the beliefs of others. That has always been my understanding of how our political system should work, and it has always informed the way I have tried to conduct my own political career. Despite what too many of today's political operatives think, politics does not have to be shrill and divisive to be effective. Too often, our politics focuses solely on winning an ideological battle without any concern for how the way the victory is achieved might affect the winner's ability to govern. If we can change that dynamic, we will change our politics, and our country, for the better.

CHAPTER TWO

Whatever Happened to the Big Umbrella?

The Republican Party is the party of the future because it is the party that draws people together, not drives them apart. Our party detests the technique of pitting group against group for cheap political advantage. Republicans view as a central principle of conduct . . . "E pluribus unum"—"Out of many—one."

DWIGHT D. EISENHOWER, 1956

It's been forty-five years since I first started to really try to figure out what my political principles were and why I considered myself a Republican. Of course, the party today is far different from the party I knew back then. That's only to be expected—the issues America faces have changed, the leadership has changed, and the country has changed. If the party hadn't changed as well, it would have ceased to exist long ago. Some of that change has been much for the good, but the more recent change in character bodes ill for the future of the GOP.

When I came of age as a Republican, the party was much more accommodating to a range of opinions within its ranks, from the far right to the moderate middle. It's hard to believe today, but at that time there were even those who proudly called themselves liberal Republicans. The various wings of the party certainly had their irritations with each other, but they nevertheless made room for one another. I was taught by my parents—staunch Republicans both—that this expansive, encompassing reach was one of the GOP's great strengths. My father referred to the party as "the big umbrella."

I can vividly recall him explaining to me for the first time that he shared a set of core of beliefs with all other Republicans, and that while there were differences within the party, every party member was connected. "It's like an umbrella," he explained. "The most important part of an umbrella is the central stick. Everything else depends on that strong central core, and although each of the ribs that radiates off the central sticks helps give shape to and supports the umbrella's canopy, without that connection to the center, they aren't of much use."

Dwight Eisenhower, Richard Nixon, Gerald Ford, Ronald Reagan, and George H. W. Bush all represented various "ribs" of the Republican Party, and none of them would have tolerated purging the party of those who didn't share their own particular brand of Republicanism. Though Reagan was viewed by many as an archconservative, he was, in fact, the master of the broad reach. Although the Republican Party throughout most of the 1980s was split, just as it is now, into its conservative and moderate wings, Reagan succeeded not only in bringing the party together, but also in attracting support from moderate and conservative Democrats. Although he also brought the religious right into the party fold, he never allowed them to dictate the terms of his presidency. Nor did he exclude or marginalize moderates, either from his administration or from the party at large. So how, in recent years, has the party allowed itself to become captive of a collection of far-right forces, whose pursuit of their own narrow agendas makes it difficult to govern and even harder to appeal to the great moderate center of the American electorate?

As I look back over my own life in the political arena, and the history of the party during that same period, I am fascinated by the conventional wisdom today that the rightward shift of the party has been the key to its electoral victories when, in fact, the legacy of the rise of the social fundamentalist wing is much more checkered.

I have been around politics literally for my entire life. My family was in many ways the embodiment of what was once known as the Republican eastern establishment. My parents, and their parents before them, had been active in the GOP since the early days of the twentieth century, holding leadership positions in the state and national party. My parents actually met at the 1932 Republican National Convention in Chicago, where their parents, John R. and Alice Bray Todd and Reeve and Kate Prentice Schley, introduced them to one another, playing matchmakers. As it turned out, 1932 wasn't a good year for the GOP, and my parents may have been the only successful pair to come out of that convention; the Republican ticket of Herbert Hoover and Charles Curtis went down to a crushing defeat, the first in a string of five Democratic presidential election victories.

For as long as I can remember, political discussions were the staple of dinner table conversation with my parents. My dad, Webster Todd (I called him Pa, and everyone else called him Web), was state party chairman in New Jersey and held official appointments from both President Eisenhower and President Nixon. My mother, Eleanor (whom I called Ma), was chair of the New Jersey Federation of Republican Women and vice chair of the Republican National Committee. Back in the mid-1950s, New Jersey's largest newspaper listed her as a woman who could one day be New Jersey's first female governor. My parents' commitment to politics was inherited by all of us children. My sister, Kate, was appointed by the first President Bush to a senior post in his administration. My brother John served on his local town council, and my brother Dan was elected to the New Jersey General Assembly and served in both the Nixon and Ford administrations.

My parents embodied the differences between the two dominant wings of the party: my father was a good deal more conservative than my politically moderate mother. They shared a devotion to the core beliefs of the party: equality of opportunity, limited government, fiscal restraint combined with lower taxes, a strong national defense. My mother, though, saw a broader role for government in helping people make the most of their potential than did my father. She believed that, within limits, government could be a force for social good—and if that cost money, it would be money well spent. My father, on the other hand, harbored deep concerns about the long-range impact of what he called runaway government spending. Perhaps it was his background as a businessman, but he thought that, for the most part, government should stay out of people's lives and that its resources should be focused on such areas as building roads and bridges, educating children, and maintaining national defense. He also believed that higher taxes only led to more government spending. No fan of Franklin Delano Roosevelt and the New Deal, he thought FDR's policies were as much designed to build the Democratic Party as they were to end the Depression. He believed that FDR's alphabet soup of programs spurred an unnecessarily massive expansion of government that became almost unstoppable. Years later, when Ronald Reagan said, "The nearest thing to eternal life we will ever see on this earth is a government program," I immediately thought of my dad and knew he would have agreed.

Even with their differences, my parents respected each other's views, and they firmly believed that moderates and conservatives both had contributions to make to the success of the party. They knew that excluding one or the other would be political foolishness. One thing they both also believed deeply, and that they taught me emphatically, was that politics was not just about winning elections; it was also about governing. They insisted that accomplishing good in a democracy requires accommodation and compromise, that politics should be about the art of the possible, a belief that is all too uncommon in our politics today. Of course, that mutual respect didn't get in the way of some very lively conversations during supper.

Every night when we'd sit down in our dining room, they'd trade thoughts about the latest issues, the current campaign, and who was up and who was down. Some of those conversations got a little warm. Pa was a tough businessman who was used to getting his way, but my mother was every bit as tough and she never gave ground just to placate him. As a girl, I heard about the time my father's father, my grandfather Todd, threw an overcooked chicken at my grandmother at Sunday dinner and demanded to know, "Who bought this lousy chicken?" My father would never have attempted such a display with my mother. Not only did he not have that kind of temper, but he also knew full well my mother would never have put up with it. Their discussions were surely lively, and neither was the slightest bit shy about their views, but they were always respectful to one another.

My parents were among those Republicans who, in late 1951, mounted a vigorous, and ultimately successful, effort to persuade Dwight Eisenhower to run for president as a Republican. Ike was so popular after the war that he'd been courted by both parties in 1948, but he had declined to run for either side. Heading into the 1952 election, he was flirting with the idea of accepting the invitation from the Republicans, but he hadn't committed; in the meanwhile, Senator Robert Taft of Ohio had positioned himself as the Republican front-runner. My parents, and many other Republicans, saw Taft as too rigidly conservative—not to mention possessed of a less-than-winning personality—and thought that if he was the nominee, the party would likely lose its sixth presidential election in a row. So they joined a steady stream of Republican Party leaders who were seeking to persuade Ike to run. In early 1952, my parents traveled to Paris to meet with Eisenhower face to face (he was then serving as commander of NATO), and they followed up with a series of letters pledging support.

When Ike finally agreed to allow his name to be appear on the New Hampshire primary ballot, both Ma and Pa redoubled their efforts to secure his nomination. The battle between the Taft and

Eisenhower camps in the party grew quite heated that spring, but at the convention Eisenhower won on the first ballot, and both sides quickly came together to deliver a decisive Republican victory, the party's first since 1928.

As I was growing up, I was intrigued by all of my parents' political activities. My father was always working behind the scenes, and mother was constantly going to one political meeting or another. She often took me along with her (my brother says it was because I was so difficult they could never get anyone to babysit for me twice), and by the time I was a teenager, I was just as fascinated with politics as were my parents. I felt as comfortable attending a political meeting as if I'd been doing it all my life— because I had.

Twenty-four years after my parents met at that 1932 Republican Convention, they took me along to my first national convention, when I was just nine years old (or as I pointed out to everyone at the time, "almost ten"). I've attended every one since—thirteen in all, including the 2004 convention in New York City—and although many of them have blurred together in my memory, that first one still stands out. That year, 1956, Ike was running for reelection, again paired with Vice President Richard Nixon. Eisenhower's popularity during his first term remained high and the convention was largely a formality. Although there had been some press speculation early in the year that Eisenhower might drop Nixon as his running mate, no one ever really took that talk seriously, and the Eisenhower-Nixon team went to San Francisco's Cow Palace for what was effectively a coronation.

Though I didn't fully appreciate at the time just how special the experience was, as I look back I realize what an extraordinary opportunity my parents gave me by taking me along to that and future conventions (I did eventually get there on my own). Because my mother was a convention official that year (as she was at many other conventions as well), she could take me anywhere in the hall—she was my equivalent of an all-access pass. Of course, at that age, the political issues at stake escaped me, but I was entranced by the excitement. I even got to meet Eisenhower himself.

On the convention's last night, when Eisenhower was to make his acceptance speech, Ma positioned me next to the stairs leading to the rostrum so I could see him up close. After his speech and the frenzy that followed, he left the platform and, spotting my mother, he stopped to thank her for all her hard work. Ma then introduced me to him. With great pride I gave him a leather golf tee holder filled with half a dozen tees, which I'd made in arts and crafts at camp earlier that summer. I will never forget how Eisenhower, who must have been eager to get back to his hotel room after a draining performance, looked me right in the eye as he thanked me and said he looked forward to putting my present to good use. I was thrilled the next day when a newspaper ran a picture of Ike waving my gift as he left San Francisco, telling reporters the next thing on his schedule was a good game of golf. Although Eisenhower would play hundreds more rounds in the coming years, I never did find out whether my tee holder had made it into the presidential golf bag. I like to think it did.

As much as I enjoyed my first convention, it certainly would have been easier for my parents to have left me home at the farm. That would have spared my mother the consternation some of her fellow convention officials felt about a photo op in which I unwittingly became the center of attraction. Several days before the convention opened, my mother was participating in a press conference called by the actor George Murphy, an active Republican who would be elected to the U.S. Senate from California eight years later. Murphy was chairing the Committee on Arrangements that year, and my mother was chair of the Subcommittee on Decorations and Music. They were both seated at a table in the front of the room with various other convention officials, while my older sister and I, along with a number of reporters, sat in the audience.

I had just returned from a visit to Disneyland and was wearing my favorite souvenir from the Magic Kingdom: a hat with a fake dagger piercing my head. Under normal circumstances, my head gear wouldn't have attracted much attention. But if you have never attended an Arrangements Committee press conference, you'll find it hard to appreciate just how boring it can be, especially if you're an experienced political reporter. So before too long, some of the reporters were practically begging me (and my hat) to join my mother in the front of the room. Without thinking—not having learned yet what a tricky thing a photo op is—I did. Flashes suddenly started going off and, needless to say, that was the picture that ran alongside all the stories about the press conference in the San Francisco papers the next day. Although Murphy thought the photo was funny, not everyone was amused. One woman on the committee later told my mother that I had acted "most inappropriately." That was the first time, but not the last, I would hear that phrase during the course of my life in politics.

My parents took me along with them to that convention—

despite the challenges of having an almost-ten-year-old in tow—because they wanted me to see firsthand the political process at work. Back then, there was no more exciting place to witness politics in action than on the floor of a national convention, where all kinds of drama could—and in those days often did—occur unexpectedly. They were far different from today's conventions, which have become little more than overly scripted, slickly packaged political infomercials, completely devoid of spontaneity. I had to chuckle when John Kerry delivered the "Help is on the way" line in his acceptance speech, and moments later, hundreds of professionally printed signs proclaiming HELP IS ON THE WAY magically appeared in the hands of the crowd. The Democrats may have believed that help was on the way, but the signs were already there. So much for spontaneity.

Walking around the Cow Palace in 1956, I had the chance to meet many of the most powerful political leaders in the country (though I had no real appreciation of who most of them were, and it didn't strike me at the time that it was at all unusual that they were all men). But what made an even bigger impression on me was the pageantry: the sheer size of the hall and the crowd, the hundreds of handmade signs and the thousands of trinkets and balloons, the bands and the funny hats people wore. All of that was exciting to a nine-year-old who realized that politics could be very interesting indeed.

One other thing I remember being fascinated by during the 1956 election season was the fact that my parents knew and respected both the Republican and Democratic candidates. My father had attended Princeton University with Adlai Stevenson, and they had maintained a casual friendship through the years. He always respected Stevenson, and I later learned that when Stevenson first ran in 1952 my father felt the country would have been well served if either man had won. After Stevenson received the Democratic nomination for the first time, my father wrote him, mixing his usual deadpan humor with his genuine respect for Stevenson, "Of course I expect to do everything possible to defeat [you], but it does give one a good feeling to know that no matter who wins in November, someone of the character of yourself or General Eisenhower will be the next President." My father took great pleasure in helping persuade Eisenhower to run and in working for his victory, but he took no delight in Stevenson's defeat. Reflecting back on the respect and affection my father readily expressed for Stevenson, I can't help but feel nostalgic for that kind of basic civility in politics. These days, there is far too much passion for demonizing our political adversaries.

Just how fierce our politics has become was brought home to me vividly as I sat in a courtroom in Dade County, Florida, during the bitter recount of 2000. I couldn't help but reflect on how different my experience had been in 1956, the first time I ever watched ballots being counted. While we were having dinner on that Election Day, my mother asked me if I wanted to go with her to watch the votes being tallied. Though I had already been bitten by the political bug, that wasn't the reason I was quick to agree to go. I knew the polls didn't close until eight that night, so if I went with her, I'd get to stay up late.

Even though my mother held a national-level position in the Republican Party, she knew very well the wisdom of Tip O'Neill's maxim that all politics is local. She spent most election nights over the years at our local polling place, the two-room firehouse just down the road from our farm in Oldwick, New Jersey. One room housed the village's one fire engine; the other was a good-size open room used for meetings, pancake breakfasts, and on every election day, for voting.

We arrived at the firehouse shortly before the polls closed. A few last-minute voters were completing their large paper ballots, and everyone who would be counting the ballots was already there. At exactly eight, the election officials closed the polls and prepared to open the ballot box. Though my mother was there as a Republican challenger, representing the party to ensure that the votes were counted fairly, everyone in the room knew her role was only a formality; they all trusted one another. These people were, after all, friends and neighbors. After witnessing the bitter Florida recount, I marvel that scenes such as that were ever really possible.

When I reflect back on my earliest political memories, I am also struck by how sad it is that so many of today's young people view politics as nothing more than a cynical game for cynical people. Voting used to be something one was proud to do, and becoming old enough to vote was an exciting rite of passage. My parents always took me along with them when they voted because they were determined to instill in me the importance of participation. I can still hear my father saying to me, as clearly as if it were yesterday, "If you don't participate, you lose your right to complain." When you're a child that makes quite an impression— the last thing you want to do is lose your right to complain.

These days, too many young people just don't bother. Barely one out of three eighteen- to twenty-five-year-olds go to the polls.

I have to say, though, that it's hard to fault young people for their disillusionment. Even in the 2004 election, in which numerous efforts were made to increase turnout among young people, voters between the ages of eighteen and thirty made up just 17 percent of those going to the polls. Overall, they make up about 24 percent of the voting age population. Their disaffection is probably partly caused by the movement away from teaching civics in our schools, but the bulk of the responsibility lies with the political parties and politicians who have contributed to the deterioration of what passes for political discussion these days.

With politics becoming ever more negative and petty, is it any wonder young people rely as much on late-night TV hosts like David Letterman, Jay Leno, Bill Maher, and Jon Stewart for the political news as they do on network news. At least the comedians intend to be laughed at. While there was no shortage of crucial and highly charged issues in the 2004 campaign, I suspect that the amount of attention paid to events thirty years in the past (before these voters were even born)—the attacks on Kerry's Vietnam service and on the president's record in the National Guard—and the sometimes questionable accuracy of the major news organizations, as highlighted by CBS's story on President Bush's National Guard service based on what turned out to be forged documents, contributed to the decision by millions of young people to stay home from the polls.

The ways in which the presidential nominating process has evolved have also taken some of the excitement and drama out of politics. In 2004, the Democrats had their candidate selected before the end of March—eight months before Election Day. By the time the conventions rolled around, there was little left to do. It's no wonder the major networks have cut their coverage to just three hours over four days.

While I remember vividly just how momentous and dramatic conventions used to be, I must admit that the drama was not always a good thing. In 1964, I attended my third national convention, held once again in San Francisco's Cow Palace, and it was one of the most lively—and portentous—in the modern history of the Republican Party. Barry Goldwater and his supporters displayed a single-mindedness that enabled them to take over the convention and win the nomination, while at the same time turning off the American people in record numbers. His supporters were unapologetically strident, which is rarely an effective way to win a general election. Looking back, it is clear that Goldwater's nomination was just the first rumbling of the full-blown battle between moderate Republicans and the new breed of much more conservative Republicans that would play out over the next forty years and is plaguing the party more today than at any previous period.

By the time of the 1964 convention, I was seventeen years old, and although many young Republican hearts belonged to Barry that year, I was a committed supporter of Nelson Rockefeller. I had liked Rockefeller since I'd started to follow him in 1960, when he made an on-again, off-again run at the Republican nomination for president. In 1960, Vice President Nixon was the strong favorite to win the Republican nomination, but from what I'd heard about Rockefeller at home, as my parents traded views, I was more drawn to Rocky, even though he couldn't seem to make up his mind whether he was in or out of the race.

Nowhere were my parents' political differences more apparent than when they talked about Nelson Rockefeller. Perhaps because my family had had a long association with the Rockefellers, their views about him were much more personal than they were with other candidates. My grandfather Todd's company built Rockefeller Center and played a major part in the restoration of Colonial Williamsburg, another huge Rockefeller project. My father and Nelson Rockefeller were each involved in their fathers' businesses, and so they had known each other long before Rocky entered the political arena. My dad's view of Rockefeller as a businessman was never very high (they had butted heads during the construction of Rockefeller Center), and he liked him even less as a politician. He thought he was too liberal—a big spender on social programs who was all too willing to raise taxes. My mother, on the other hand, was a strong Rockefeller supporter. Not only did she like his progressive approach to social problems, but she was also clearly attracted by his personality and charisma.

Nelson Rockefeller was one of those people who seem to enjoy everything they do, no matter what it is. His enthusiasm for life was infectious—at least my mother and I caught the bug. In the end, however, Rockefeller never really came close to denying the nomination to Nixon, who went on to face John F. Kennedy in one of the closest and most exciting presidential campaigns ever.

Though I'd rooted for Rockefeller as a candidate in 1960, I have to admit I hadn't yet developed any deep understanding of the political issues being debated. I was about to turn fourteen that year, and what mattered most to me at the convention was being assigned as page to the actor Efrem Zimbalist, Jr. I *loved* him on *77 Sunset Strip*, and was determined to be the most attentive and

43

useful page anyone had ever had. I stuck to him like glue. He couldn't shake me. Finally, in what must have been a desperate attempt to get at least a few minutes of privacy, he sent me off to look for a pack of cigarettes. I'm not sure he even smoked.

Between the summer of 1960 and the 1964 convention, I'd had the opportunity to get some distance from the influence of my parents. Though I wasn't happy about it at the time, that distance did help me formulate my own views about politics. In the fall of 1960, I found myself away from home for the first time, and I didn't have the benefit of dinnertime conversations with my parents to keep me abreast of the latest news from the campaign trail. Earlier that year, as I was getting ready to begin high school, my parents had decided to send me to the Foxcroft School, a girls' boarding school in Middleburg, Virginia. My mother and my sister were both Foxcroft alums and they loved the time they had spent there. I did not. The school was organized along the lines of a military academy, complete with demerits, marching and rifle drills, and room inspections. Having been raised essentially as an only child (my sister and brothers were all away at boarding school by the time I was riding the bus to second grade), I was used to having the run of the farm. At Foxcroft, I felt as if I had been confined to quarters. Looking back, it would be fair to say I was a spoiled brat. So it was not surprising that when I had to confront the regimentation of Foxcroft, I was not happy.

Despite massive homesickness, I learned many things about myself while away at school, including that I was not one to accept rules for their own sake. The most important thing I discovered about myself, though, was how much I missed that daily dose of politics with my parents at dinner. It seemed to me that my fellow students hardly cared at all about the campaign (although just because they didn't care as much as I did, didn't mean they didn't care at all). After spending the first thirteen years of my life in a home where political discussion was as much a part of our daily lives as milking the cows, I couldn't believe that there were actually places in the world where people didn't live and breathe politics.

My mother tried to help me feel involved by sending me autographs of various politicians my parents had met on the campaign trail. At the time, I didn't much appreciate her gesture—it made me miss home even more. But one of those slips of paper included a bit of advice that I have never forgotten. It was from the governor of Michigan—a man whose son Mitt is now serving as governor of Massachusetts. He wrote, "To Christie, Luck is when opportunity meets preparedness, Sincerely, George Romney."

At the start of the election year in 1960, I considered myself a Republican (as I always had) but only because that's what my parents were. Away from their daily influence, I had to begin to think for myself about the two parties, and I worked hard at trying to formulate my own sense about what they stood for, and also to discover what I believed. While I may not have been spending every day with my parents, their influence still had a strong effect on my thinking, and I found myself blending their two approaches to government. I shared my father's fiscal conservatism but leavened it with the social concerns my mother held.

Forty years before Karen Hughes coined the phrase "compassionate conservative," the Republican Party I first consciously embraced respected the importance of a balanced, socially concerned approach to the role of government. It seemed to me that the Democrats had decided that more government was the solution to every problem. Republicans, however, feared that government's reach could actually prevent Americans from reaching their potential. Punishing taxes, unreasonable regulation, and massive social welfare programs could rob people of initiative and drive, inadvertently worsening problems they were meant to solve. Yet the party also reflected clearly—more clearly then than now—the view that government had a responsibility for those who, through no fault of their own, were not able to claim their piece of all that America had to offer.

It seemed to me then, and still does today, that Republicans had more faith in the individual American, whereas Democrats put their faith in the ability of elected elites to define and determine what's best for average Americans. The traditional Republican approach struck me as more respectful of people; the Democratic approach seemed somewhat arrogant. Ironically, that difference isn't as clear-cut anymore. Now the platform of the Republican Party seeks to assert government control over all sorts of personal behavior, an intrusiveness most Republicans would have once opposed. We've come a long way since 1960 as a party, and I think that despite the 2004 victory, in a very real sense we've lost our way.

The leaders of the party when I came of age as a Republican were pragmatic believers in government's ability to help address the range of social problems America was facing. Dwight Eisenhower established the Department of Health, Education and Welfare and warned America about the dangers of a military-industrial complex. Richard Nixon called himself a practical liberal when he first ran for Congress in 1946 and was never accepted as "one of our own" by the right wing of the Republican Party. Nelson Rockefeller's enlightened civil rights policies as governor of New York were a model for the nation. I was proud that my party—the party of Lincoln—was home to Edward W. Brooke of Massachusetts, the first African American ever elected to the United States Senate by popular vote, and to Margaret Chase Smith, the first woman to have her name placed in nomination for president by either major political party. These were the leaders of the Republican Party and the standard-bearers of the party's legacy that I was drawn to when I made a conscious decision to become a Republican. Sometimes I wonder whether any of them would find a home in today's Grand Old Party.

My father's description of the Republican Party as a big umbrella fit the party in 1960, but in the presidential campaign of 1964, with the zealous insurgency of Goldwater and his supporters, that inclusive, expansive philosophy came increasingly under siege. I'll never forget my firsthand taste at the convention that year of just how bitter (and self-destructive) that intraparty battle would become.

When the 1964 election season rolled around, my choice of a candidate was clear, given the political convictions I'd come to in the preceding years. Though ours was a house divided when it came to Nelson Rockefeller, I was still a huge Rocky supporter. Not only did I think he was a gifted politician—charismatic with an unexpected common touch—I especially liked his deep and clear sense of social justice. Despite being born to enormous privilege, he showed a genuine concern, not simply for those less fortunate than him (which was just about everybody), but also for those society had truly left behind—the poor, the uneducated, and the victims of racial prejudice. People responded to him, and he to them.

I found Goldwater, on the other hand, to be scary, as, it would turn out, did most Americans. Where Rockefeller seemed possessed by joy, Goldwater appeared completely mirthless to me. He used what struck me as almost apocalyptic rhetoric that, while red meat for his strongest supporters, unnerved mainstream America. The two could not have been further apart—in outlook or in temperament.

Rockefeller, a New Yorker, was the leading member of the so-called eastern elite of the party (soon to be pejoratively dubbed Rockefeller Republicans). Goldwater was a rawboned Arizonan, the standard-bearer of the rising western conservative wing of the party that was determined to put those easterners in their place. Although Goldwater saw government as the enemy of the people; Rockefeller saw it as their ally. Goldwater pushed for massive increases in defense spending, whereas Rockefeller advocated investing in social programs. Goldwater voted against the Civil Rights Act of 1964; Rockefeller supported it. Their battle for the nomination opened fissures between the moderate and the conservative wings of the party that have grown into major fault lines.

From the beginning, Rockefeller's campaign was an uphill battle. Goldwater's supporters were unusually zealous, and they were able to match their zeal with a well-organized grass roots organizational effort. I first encountered the Goldwater extremists at a Young Republican meeting in my home county in the summer of 1964, prior to the Republican National Convention. The local YRs had been taken over by a group of conservative activists who called themselves, apparently without irony, the Rat Finks. At that meeting, one of the Rat Finks stood up and, looking straight at me, warned that the club had to watch out for "communist-fascists" who were trying to infiltrate the organization. His statement made two things quite obvious to me. First, that he needed to take an entry-level course in political theory. Second, that a so-called eastern elitist like me was not welcome in a group that didn't see the party as a big umbrella. They cared more about taking it over than about winning the general election. That attitude was famously expressed by Goldwater himself during the campaign, when his response to the charge that he couldn't win in November was to declare, "First let's take over the party. Then we'll go from there."

By the time the convention rolled around, it was clear that nobody was going to stop Goldwater. I was a page again, this time for the New Jersey delegation (I'm sure if Efrem Zimbalist, Jr., had been there, he would have made sure I received an assignment far away from him). Before the convention began, Rockefeller had bowed out of the race, but in keeping with a tradition meant to bring the party together after a tough fight, he was given the opportunity to speak. I'll never forget the mayhem when he took the podium. The Goldwater partisans started booing and heckling him with such vehemence that they totally drowned him out. But Rocky would not be deterred. I can still vividly see him standing there defiantly, telling the crowd that he had been given five minutes to speak and he was going to use every one of them, whether they liked it or not. I saw one of the members of the New Jersey delegation actually stand on his chair and spit at Rockefeller (even though they were hundreds of feet apart). I was both repulsed by the crudeness of the gesture and bemused by its futility. At the time, that act seemed to me an omen of where this new brand of Republicanism would take the party later that fall.

I will never forget the closing night of the convention when Goldwater gave his acceptance speech. He almost lifted the roof off the hall. The pent-up enthusiasm of the Goldwater delegates was unleashed in all its fury—and at no time more so than when Goldwater delivered a now famous line that so energized his supporters and so disturbed everyone else in the party and in the country: "Extremism in the defense of liberty is no vice. Moderation in the pursuit of justice is no virtue." That line brought down the house and finished his campaign almost before it had even started. Goldwater lost to Lyndon Johnson in the worst defeat of any Republican presidential candidate in thirty years.

It's clear to me now that the Goldwater campaign appealed to the crudest instincts of the electorate—fear, anger, and division—and, as a result, to a very limited portion of the nation's voters. After the horror of the Kennedy assassination, which many at the time felt was the result of a right-wing conspiracy, the American people were in no mood for an archconservative firebrand. The Democrats took full advantage of this climate, portraying Goldwater as Neanderthal on the domestic front and cavalier in foreign policy. Goldwater had made some all-too-casual references to the possible use of nuclear weapons in Europe to repel a hypothetical Soviet attack, which made him seem reckless and irresponsible. The Democrats were quick to exploit his ill-chosen words to fan the public's fears. Their most memorable attack on Goldwater was a TV ad that ran just once. It pictured a young girl standing in a field, counting as she plucked the petals off a daisy. Suddenly, her voice was replaced by the almost mechanical voice of a man counting down for a nuclear launch. The ad ended showing a giant nuclear explosion with a voice-over of President Johnson saying, "These are the stakes: to make a world in which all of God's children can live, or to go into the dark. We must either love each other, or we must die." Goldwater's name was never mentioned, but the effect was devastating. Even Ronald Reagan's brilliant stump speech on Goldwater's behalf—which was run as a paid ad just a week before Election Day—was not enough to rescue the Republican ticket. It did, however, help launch Reagan on his own political career.

A key part of Goldwater's campaign plan was to wrest the Solid South away from the Democrats. For fully a century, since the end of the Civil War and Reconstruction, the Democrats had held an electoral lock on the South. Yet as the 1960s unfolded, the Solid South began to show some stress fractures. By 1964, the increasing dominance of northern liberals in the Democratic Party, capped by Lyndon Johnson's push for the passage of the Civil Rights Act of 1964, encouraged Goldwater to try to break the Democrats' hold on the South. What became known as the Republicans' Southern Strategy first took root in the Goldwater camp.

Goldwater's Southern Strategy was perhaps best described by New York's senator Jacob Javits, who in 1965 identified it as "the encouragement given by some Republicans to the wooing of the 'White backlash' vote, which meant copying the demagogic tactics patented by many Southern Democrats." In plain language, this meant that Goldwater consciously catered to the deep resentment that many white southern Democrats felt about the federal government's efforts to advance civil rights, especially the mandate to integrate schools and other public places.

Interestingly, prior to 1964, Goldwater had a good record on civil rights. He had voted for federal civil rights bills earlier in his Senate career, had been instrumental in desegregating the National Guard in his home state of Arizona, and he had done away with segregation in the chain of stores his family ran. Despite that record, when the 1964 Civil Rights Act came up for a vote—in the midst of his presidential campaign—he voted against it (a position in which he was joined by virtually every southern Democrat in the Senate). This won him considerable support from many white southerners who had come to view Lyndon Johnson as a traitor to their region. At the time, Goldwater offered a closely reasoned justification of his vote against the bill on constitutional grounds, but he clearly had other motives as well. In the years since, Goldwater supporters have tended to soft-pedal that vote, but as David Eisenhower (Ike's grandson) recently observed, Goldwater knew how his vote would be perceived by white voters in the South and was willing to benefit from that perception, so any evaluation of that vote must include holding him responsible for the perception he helped create.

In a perverse way, the Southern Strategy worked: for the first time since 1880, a Republican was able to carry the heart of the Deep South: Alabama, Georgia, Louisiana, Mississippi, and South Carolina. Only Dwight Eisenhower had been able to break the absolute lock the Democrats had held on those states—by carrying Louisiana in 1956. Other than that single victory in that one state, no Republican had carried any of those states in the twenty-one presidential elections before 1964.

However, in Goldwater's quest to pry the Solid South away from the Democrats, he apparently forgot that there were forty-five other states in the Union. He ended up carrying only one other state—his home state of Arizona. And his defeat was not his alone. The Republican Party suffered heavy losses all the way down the ballot, losing thirty-seven seats in the House, two in the Senate, and more than five hundred in state legislatures. In the end, Goldwater's Southern Strategy did not immediately translate into broad Republican success in that region. In 1968, the Republicans again lost the South, as they did again in 1976 (Nixon carried the South in 1972, as he did every other state in the union except Massachusetts), and it wasn't until the veteran Democratic senators and House members began to retire or die in the 1970s that Republicans began to win congressional seats in the South. There's no doubt, however, that Goldwater's efforts to loosen the Democrats' lock on the Solid South planted the seeds of future GOP dominance in the region.

A legacy of the Southern Strategy was that it played to regressive and racist sentiments, and thereby tainted the party with a reputation it has been unable to shake. Even though overwhelming majorities of Republicans in the Congress had voted for the Civil Rights Act of 1964, the party had nominated one of the few Republicans to vote against it, and that's what black voters seemed to remember. In 1960, one third of black voters supported the Republican ticket, but just 6 percent of black voters supported Goldwater in 1964, an erosion of more than 80 percent. In the forty years since, no Republican presidential candidate has ever received more than 15 percent of the African American vote.

Try as the Goldwater people might (and some of them are still trying today), his loss could not be blamed on the moderates in the party. Even in the face of the rancor of the Goldwater campaign, the moderates who lost the battle in San Francisco did not sit out the fall campaign. In contrast with many of today's social fundamentalists and the others in the Republican Party who refuse to support Republicans who don't share their rigid views, moderate Republicans in 1964 campaigned hard for Goldwater. Richard Nixon made more 150 appearances in 36 states. Nelson Rockefeller's decision to support Goldwater cost him the support of baseball legend Jackie Robinson, one of Rocky's strongest boosters during the fight for the nomination. Even Pennsylvania governor Bill Scranton, who had mounted a last-ditch effort in San Francisco to deny Goldwater the nomination, got behind Goldwater because, as he explained in a speech in New Jersey that fall, "Those of us who had strong feelings about what kind of a political party the Republican Party ought to be, have an obligation to continue to stand for that kind of party. But we can do this best by staying inside the Party. You don't help your party by leaving it. You don't evolve a progressive Republican Party by deserting it. And you don't help the Party by refusing to support its duly nominated candidate." Those are words I wish today's social fundamentalist Republicans would hear.

When I returned home from San Francisco in 1964, terribly disappointed by the results of the convention, I pasted in my scrapbook a copy of the platform—which, at the time, I read as a handbook for disaster—and somewhat bitterly wrote above it,

"The Goldwater Declaration." Now, going back and reading that platform (a short, simple twenty-seven-page pamphlet that asserts broad Republican principles), I find I would be far more comfortable running on it than I would be on the platforms adopted by the Republican Party in more recent years.

Ironically, Barry Goldwater would be considered a moderate today, if not in temperament at least in many of his principles. He spoke out as a strong supporter of a woman's right to choose and believed that banning homosexuals from serving in America's armed forces was "just stupid." In the mid-1990s, I visited Goldwater's ranch for a fund-raiser for the Republican candidate for governor of Arizona, a moderate named Fife Symington. It was the first time I'd met "Mr. Conservative," and I have to admit I found him charming. We discussed the gays in the military issue, and I remember him saying to me, "When you're under fire, you don't care who the guy on your left or right likes to sleep with. You just want to know that they're good shots."

Today, those positions on abortion and gays in the military are dismissed by many of the Republican social fundamentalists as the confused ramblings of an old man. On the contrary, they flowed from one of the simple declarative statements of principle on which Goldwater ran in 1964, contained in that year's platform: "We . . . pledge the maximum restraint of Federal intrusion unto matters more productively left to the individual." Those words are echoed in a column he wrote in 1993 for the *Washington Post:* "The conservative movement, to which I subscribe, has as one its basic tenets the belief that government should stay out of people's private lives. Government governs best when it governs least—and stays out of the impossible task of legislating morality."

On these two issues alone, he would fail the same right-wing litmus test that I fail and which has cost me the support of many conservative members of my own party.

The story of how the Republicans were able to come back just four years after Goldwater's devastating defeat and reclaim the presidency behind Richard Nixon is also, ironically, a story of the costs of extremism. Many factors contributed to Richard Nixon's win in 1968, but the country's descent into widespread social disorder during the Johnson presidency and the increasing radicalism of the Democratic Party—displayed so graphically at the 1968 Democratic National Convention in Chicago—certainly played major, if not decisive, roles.

As the carnage in Vietnam escalated, American cities began erupting in violence, college campuses descended into chaos, and political assassinations rocked the United States to its very core. In the midst of all that turmoil, the Republican Party began, quite deliberately, to rebuild and reclaim its more moderate place in the political spectrum. In the 1966 midterm elections, the GOP picked up 47 seats in the House of Representatives, 3 in the United States Senate, 8 governorships, and 540 state legislative seats—and that was before opposition to Vietnam began to seriously damage LBJ's presidency. Those victories were distributed across the United States, and they signaled that although the Party had been bloodied by 1964, it was unbowed.

Shortly after I returned from the Goldwater convention, I started what would be four very happy years at Wheaton College in Norton, Massachusetts. In 1964, most college campuses were still peaceful—the "sixties" had not yet really started. Even as the politics of protest heated up in the coming years, most college campuses were largely isolated from the unrest, and Wheaton was among them. I attended only one protest during my four years at college, and it wasn't about Vietnam—it was to oppose efforts to restrict access to information about birth control. That's not to say that we didn't follow what was going on in Vietnam—we did. During my sophomore year, in the spring of 1966, I was one of two student members on a campuswide student-faculty panel discussion politely titled "Vietnam: Where Do We Go from Here??" I supported the war effort; I felt what we were doing—trying to prevent the expansion of communism throughout Southeast Asia—was in our national interest. In retrospect, I still believe we were in Vietnam for a worthy, even noble, cause, even if our strategy for engagement was flawed, as it so clearly was. The major lesson that Vietnam holds for America is that we must never go to war without a plan to win, not just the war but also the peace—a lesson reinforced by the challenges in Iraq after the fall of Baghdad.

Though the Wheaton campus was never rocked by protests and violence, by the time I was finishing my senior year and the 1968 campaign was heating up, the intensity of political upheaval was pervading American life. To me and my friends at college, as to so many other Americans, politics in the country seemed to be coming unglued. The antiwar Democrat Gene McCarthy drove LBJ from the race with a near win in the first-in-the-nation New Hampshire primary. Then, just eight weeks later, Bobby Kennedy, who had become the front-runner for the nomination, was gunned down in a Los Angeles hotel kitchen right after claiming victory in the California primary, only weeks after Dr. Martin Luther King, Jr., had been assassinated in Memphis. Meanwhile,

George C. Wallace repudiated his party with his own campaign as a states' rights (read *segregationist*) candidate, eventually winning four of the five southern states that Goldwater had carried in 1964. The Democratic convention in Chicago was the most contentious and violent in American history as protesters and police clashed in the streets surrounding the convention site while the party tried to conduct its business in the midst of enormous upheaval inside the hall.

In contrast, the Republicans that year avoided the internecine warfare that tore apart the Democrats. Richard Nixon mounted what would become known as one of the great political comebacks in twentieth-century American politics. In the four years since Goldwater had gone down in flames, Nixon had laid all the groundwork necessary for his political resurrection. He had worked tirelessly for Republican candidates in the 1966 midterm elections, and the huge GOP victories that year were attributed, in no small measure, to Nixon's efforts. In addition, he had put together a very effective grassroots organization. The media talked about a "new Nixon"—more mature, more measured, more moderate, and more confident than the Nixon who had lost the presidency in 1960 and the governorship of California in 1962. Nixon, a native Californian, knew how to appeal to the more conservative voters in the South and West without alienating the moderate wing of the party, as Goldwater had. Throughout the primary season, Republican voters showed they were willing to give Nixon another chance—he had not only earned their trust and support, he had also managed to bring the party back together. Nixon succeeded in bringing together the moderates, the traditional conservatives, and the Goldwater Republicans, all of whom found a place in his campaign and contributed to his victory in November.

I learned a valuable lesson in party unity that year. Nixon did not cruise to the nomination unopposed; he first had to fend off several challengers, including Michigan governor George Romney and Nelson Rockefeller. In the weeks before the Republican convention, I was once again an ardent and involved Rocky supporter. Had Nixon been running today, the string of primary victories he won starting in New Hampshire would have sealed the nomination long before the convention, but in 1968, winning primaries did yet not guarantee that a candidate would then capture the presidential nomination. Party leaders still controlled delegations in several dozen states. My fellow Rocky supporters and I held out hope that if he could secure endorsements from enough uncommitted delegates, he might be able to deny Nixon a first-ballot majority, after which all bets were off. It didn't work out that way. When Rockefeller lost again, I was so disappointed that I felt like spending the rest of the campaign on the sidelines.

Days after returning home from the convention, I wrote to Massachusetts Senator Edward Brooke, a man I had come to admire and respect during my college years in his home state, to ask for his advice about what I should do. He very generously wrote back to me just a few weeks later, saying that while Nixon and Agnew were not his first choice either, he would "actively support the ticket with conviction and with enthusiasm." That taught me a lesson about party unity I still value. In the end, I volunteered for the Nixon campaign. For reasons that are still not clear, I was made New Jersey coordinator of Italian-Americans for Nixon-Agnew. When Nixon won, carrying New Jersey for the

Republicans for the first time since 1956 (I like to think it was the Italian-American vote that put us over the top), I began to think about what to do next. I had graduated from college and I needed a job—so among the options I explored was a job in Washington.

As I look back from the vantage point of more than thirty years, it is clear to me that there were two keys to victory in 1968. Although many still attribute the Democrats' narrow loss solely to the chaos that so divided the country, I believe that the combination of Republican unity and the moderate face the party presented to the electorate made the real difference. Nixon lost four of the six states that Goldwater had carried in 1968 (they went for Wallace), but he won in twenty-nine of the forty-four states that Goldwater lost.

Nixon's well-known formula for success for Republican candidates (run to the right in the primary; then return to the center for the general election) carried over to his presidency. Though he had attracted the support of the conservative wing of the party, he did not allow his presidency to be controlled by it. By any standard, Nixon governed largely as a moderate. He inaugurated détente with the Soviet Union and opened the door to the People's Republic of China; he sought to create a national health insurance program; he created the Environmental Protection Agency; he instituted affirmative action in the awarding of federal contracts and completed the long overdue desegregation of the public schools in the South; he even increased funding for the National Endowment for the Arts and for public television.

Though Americans today tend to think of Nixon as a conservative, the true believers in the conservative wing of the party at the time never thought so. An Ohio congressman named John

Ashbrook spoke for many of them with his quixotic primary challenge from the right. Ashbrook's declaration that he was "an American first, a conservative second, and a Republican third" attracted the support of such leading conservatives as William F. Buckley and Phyllis Schlafly (but not that of Reagan or Goldwater, who backed the president). Following Ashbrook's unsuccessful attempt, another very conservative congressman, John Schmitz of California, left the party and launched his own, a third-party bid for the White House. After Nixon's landslide re-election victory in 1972 (carrying forty-nine states and winning more than 60 percent of the popular vote), he was determined to create a New Republican Majority. Watergate intervened, and the Nixon presidency—and any plans for building a new majority—came to an abrupt halt.

The fallout from Watergate provided the opening conservatives needed to reenergize their march to take over the party. As they searched for a new standard-bearer, they found him in Ronald Reagan. Reagan had impressed them in 1964 with his efforts on Goldwater's behalf, and two years later he won a stunning victory for himself, being elected in a landslide as governor of California while running on an unapologetic conservative platform. Philosophically, Reagan was a Goldwater conservative, but where Goldwater made people uneasy, Reagan had a knack for putting them at ease. Almost immediately after he was elected, talk about a future presidential candidacy started to percolate. He had even toyed with the idea of challenging Nixon in 1968 for the Republican nomination before realizing his time had not yet come.

In 1976, however, Reagan did decide to run, and he came

within a whisker of denying President Ford (who had ascended to the presidency when Nixon resigned) the GOP nomination. Ford's subsequent loss to Jimmy Carter, an obscure southern governor, followed by the failure of Carter's presidency, gave the old Goldwater conservatives the added boost they needed.

In retrospect, it's clear that the Carter years played to the strength of the building conservative movement. From the conservative point of view, it was, after all, the moderate Republicans who had lost the presidency to the disastrous Jimmy Carter. Only a true conservative like Ronald Reagan, they argued, could now rescue the Republican Party from its moderate members and save America from the Democrats.

Reagan's prodigious political skills played an indispensable role. Where Carter talked of America's malaise, Reagan lifted our spirits. Where Carter fretted about a nation in decline, Reagan saw America as a shining city on a hill. Reagan also perceived the burgeoning power of the up-and-coming religious right and shrewdly courted its support. By the time the 1980 convention was over, Reagan had secured the party's presidential nomination, and the conservatives were in control.

The conservative wing of the party in 1980 was much different from what it is today. In 1980, Reagan knew he had to hold the party together, so he picked George H. W. Bush—a moderate Republican if ever there was one—to be his vice president. He also knew that in building his winning coalition by reaching out to the religious right, he had to be careful not to push away the rest of the electorate. His success in creating a bastion of Reagan Democrats proves how successfully he managed that feat. While he remained true to his core principles, he also knew how to compromise to get things done, and he never engaged in internecine warfare. Reagan practiced what he called the eleventh commandment: "Thou shalt not speak ill of thy fellow Republicans."

Too many of the people who hold enormous influence in today's Republican Party seem to have forgotten that Reagan wisdom. Many conservative leaders withheld their support for George H. W. Bush's reelection in 1992 because they believed he was not sufficiently conservative, even though they had to know that doing so would help elect Bill Clinton. When Bush lost, many of them rejoiced. I read that members of one right-wing group known as the Third Generation reportedly celebrated Bush 41's defeat by carrying into a party a rubber-mask likeness of the recently defeated president's head on a platter festooned with blood-red crepe paper.

Even during the past four years, with the most socially conservative president of my lifetime in the White House, many of the ideological zealots in the party complained that the president wasn't sufficiently conservative. Throughout 2004, hardly a week went by without a prominent conservative writing that he or she couldn't vote for the president because he wasn't conservative enough. When the prime-time speaking schedule was announced for the 2004 Republican convention, and it included so many moderate Republicans, judging by the reaction of the social fundamentalists, you would think that Howard Dean and Hillary Clinton had been invited to speak.

The leaders of the various conservative factions in the party today also fail to appreciate something Ronald Reagan knew and practiced: how to truly listen to what others say. The importance of listening was a lesson I learned for myself after I had landed my second job in Washington, at the Republican National Committee in 1969. Before I went to the RNC, I had worked for Donald Rumsfeld in the Office of Economic Opportunity. During my brief stint at the OEO, my duties were largely limited to administrative support. I was eager to make a more substantial contribution and was on the lookout for how I might create that opportunity. Early that spring, a perfect opportunity arose. The new chairman of the Republican National Committee, Rogers C. B. Morton, was holding a lunch for all the state party chairmen. My father was then the Republican chairman in New Jersey, so I went to the lunch to see him—and also to try to speak with Chairman Morton about an idea I had been kicking around since I had first gone off to college.

When I had arrived at Wheaton five years earlier, I noticed right away how few young people identified with the Republican Party. Many of my peers had been drawn to the youthful image projected by the Kennedy administration and called themselves Democrats, but when I discussed politics with them, I found that their political views were actually not much different from my own. That led me to wonder what it was about the Republican Party that limited its appeal to young people. As I grew older, I came to realize that the party had the same problem appealing to the elderly and to African Americans. The more I thought about this challenge, the more I thought that the only way to find out why we were doing so poorly with those groups was to ask them, and to listen—really listen—to what they had to say. So when I met Chairman Morton at the luncheon, I pitched him an idea, namely that the RNC send a staffer (me, for example) out into the country to listen to groups of youth, blacks, and seniors talk about what political issues were most important to them and what they thought about the Republican Party. I proposed to use that information to improve the party's outreach efforts to these voters. Within a few weeks, I found myself on the staff of the Republican National Committee, in charge of what we had named the Listening Program. The insights I gleaned from that effort have never left me. They reinforced my feeling that there is far more that unites us as a people than divides us, and I still believe that, though surely the partisan divide is as wide today as it has ever been in my lifetime.

Landing that job at the RNC also gave me one of my first exposures to just how far women had to go to be taken seriously in politics. A few weeks after I started at the RNC, the New Jersey State Republican Committee (from which my father had, only the month before, retired as chairman) took note of my new post in their newsletter, writing, "Good luck and good learning to Chris Todd who is doing her political thing at National Headquarters where she is an assistant to the first assistant . . . She's papa bear's pretty bundle of charm, wit and political savvy." The condescending tone of that tidbit retains its capacity to rankle even now.

Fortunately, the attitude at the RNC was quite a bit more evolved. When I reported for work, I was both surprised and pleased that the average age of my colleagues was about twenty-five. Chairman Morton was definitely interested in finding ways that Republicans could appeal to young voters. The intense passions of the antiwar movement did not, in either his or the White House's opinion, reflect the views of the majority, either of the country or of youth. If they had believed that young people were unalterably opposed to Republicans and the administration, President Nixon would probably not have advocated the lowering of the voting age from twenty-one to eighteen.

Over the course of the following year, I traveled, mostly alone but sometimes with one other staffer, to more than a dozen cities stretching from Hartford to Los Angeles, Portland to Galveston, and numerous places in between, talking to groups of young people, African Americans, and the elderly. The interesting experiences were many, and I learned a great deal about views on both the left and right of the political spectrum. In Chicago, we had a midnight meeting with members of a gang called the Black Disciples. If I had been less naive, I probably would have been frightened of going into an inner-city high-crime area late at night to meet with gang members to hear their views on the Republican Party. As is often the case in human nature, since I didn't realize I should be afraid, I wasn't. The meeting started with some rather vociferous posturing by several of the gang's leaders, but once we got past that, we had an excellent session. I also vividly recall a meeting at the University of Colorado, where the students in attendance were extremely hostile to the administration's policy in Vietnam. Finding opposition to the war on an activist campus was no surprise, but I did come away impressed that the root of their anger about the war was frustration at what they saw as a failure of America's promise to be a beacon of peace and freedom to the rest of the world.

In Oregon, a group of reactionaries affiliated with the ultra-far-right John Birch Society found out we were coming to town and tried to dominate the public meeting. They had no trouble making their voices heard, but their arguments met with less success. They won very few, if any, converts that night.

During a trip to Texas, I was exposed to the most disturbing example of racism I had ever personally experienced. My host in Galveston was a man whose name I'll never forget: Loveland Johnson, a young African American from Houston who was working with me on our visit. Since we had some time to kill before our meetings that evening, Loveland suggested we take a ride on the Galveston-Bolivar Ferry, which makes a scenic six-mile round-trip across the bay. We were enjoying the ride when we began to notice a group of white men staring hard in our direction, then talking heatedly among themselves. It soon became obvious that they were offended by the sight of a young white woman in the company of a young black man. I have to admit that I felt afraid, and so did Loveland. When we returned to the dock after the trip, we were met by another black Texas Republican Party member who told us that the party headquarters had received some telephoned threats about our meeting later that night. The threat of violence was so real, I reluctantly canceled that night's listening session. I was not about to put Loveland or anyone else in danger.

What I find most interesting now about what I heard during my year on the road with the Listening Program is how relevant so much of it is to today's Republican Party. In a memo I wrote in April 1970, I reported that the blacks we met with "don't feel Republicans really want them and this has been reinforced by the lack of recruitment efforts for blacks and the lack of rewards for those who are in the Party . . . but the Republican attitudes of bringing the government back to the people, and fiscal integrity are attractive." With respect to senior citizens, I reported that "what they were really looking for was some evidence of concern for them and recognition that they had many problems that set them apart from other groups." Regarding students and youth, my memo found that "they want to be heard and to have some respect shown for their opinions." I also found they were concerned about the environment and the plight of the inner cities.

What is even more interesting is what the people we listened to said for themselves. One African American man in Harlem said, "I think the Republican Party has got an opportunity and doesn't even know it. That is to rebuild, and it is possible if they had the talent around. They could take the blacks away from the Democrats." Those words are every bit as true today as they were in 1969.

The potential to bring such voters into the party still exists, but as long as Republican primaries are contests to find the most conservative candidates around, without regard to their ability to appeal to the broader electorate, that potential will remain unfulfilled. Of course, strategists like Karl Rove have always understood the need to win, which explains why, in 2004, the White House supported Arlen Specter in the bitter Pennsylvania primary, even though many of the president's conservative allies were working hard to defeat Specter. It's not, after all, good politics to ignore the nearly 40 percent of voters who identify themselves as moderates—people who are, by definition, alienated by the extreme positions taken by both parties on a variety of hot-button issues. Republican leaders, by not listening, are creating a gap between themselves and a large portion of the electorate.

Today's social fundamentalists have succeeded in achieving the goal Barry Goldwater laid out in 1964: "First, let's take over the party." By pressing their hard-line views on a key set of social issues so zealously, the social fundamentalists within the party have repudiated not just the true legacy of the Republican Party, but also of the Reagan revolution, widening the divide within the party as well as in the country as a whole. These doctrinaire positions on a handful of key issues, including abortion, stem cell research, and marriage, have been tearing our party, and our country, further and further apart.

The Pew Research Center for the People and the Press found in their report *The 2004 Political Landscape,* "This remains a country that is almost evenly divided politically yet further apart than ever in its political values." I believe that is a direct result of the fact that political strategists in both parties have turned their attention in recent years to solidifying and then turning out their bases. The success Republican political operatives have had in winning elections by turning out larger proportions of smaller parts of the electorate have certainly made them seem like geniuses. I believe that if the Republican Party is going to become a true majority party in America, not just one with the slimmest margin of victory, it has to start looking now beyond the base. It has to broaden its appeal by keeping those Republicans whose moderate positions have made them outcasts and by seeking to bring in those moderate independents and conservative Democrats who have been wandering in the political wilderness in search of a party in which they can feel at home.

Lee Atwater used to talk about the Republican Party as a big tent with room enough for all those who shared its basic beliefs.

I've always preferred my father's analogy—the big umbrella—because it more clearly suggests the importance of one strong central set of beliefs from which the various ribs radiate to hold up the entire party. Today's Republican Party, however, seems more to me like a closed umbrella, with room underneath its canopy only for that rigid central shaft. It's time for moderates to lead an effort to unfurl the party's big umbrella and make room, once again, for all those who share in the fundamental principles for which the party has long stood, putting an end to the narrow litmus tests that are dividing our party and which could ultimately lead it back into the political wilderness.

CHAPTER THREE

The Party Within the Party

[L]et me say this about our friends who are now Republicans but who do not identify themselves as conservatives: I want the record to show that I do not view the new revitalized Republican Party as one based on a principle of exclusion. After all, you do not get to be a majority party by searching for groups you won't associate or work with.

RONALD REAGAN, 1977

There is no doubt in my mind that the rise of the social fundamentalist wing of the GOP is a serious threat to the long-term competitiveness of the Republican Party. It is also making it almost impossible for the party to develop a program for governing. The social fundamentalists could even cause the party to lose its hold on the Congress and the White House before the end of this decade.

The leaders of the social fundamentalists have become so single-minded that I think it's fair to say they are *in* the Republican Party but not *of* the Republican Party. Since the only Republicans the leaders of this faction will support are those who endorse their narrow social agenda without exception, they are, in a very real sense, a party within the party; they have become the tail wagging the dog.

It's clear that the motivating force behind the efforts of the social fundamentalists in the political arena is their religious faith. I respect that. My own religious faith has always been very important to me. America was founded by religious men and women who, in our founding charter, asked the blessings of God on their new nation. Over the course of our history, our nation has been greatly enriched by the contribution religion has made to our national life. But it is equally true that in this country, as set forth in the Constitution, we maintain a distance between our civil and religious institutions. That distance has served us well because it has helped us avoid the overheated religious divisions which have, throughout history, divided nations and peoples. I would never seek to exclude people of any religious faith from participating in our civic life. But neither should people of faith seek to impose their religious tenets, through the instruments of government, on their fellow citizens. Such efforts are simply inconsistent with America's traditions, as well as those of the Republican Party.

That's why it was disturbing to many Americans to see the attempts the Bush campaign made in 2004 to turn America's religious institutions into arms of its political machine. The campaign's request to supporters to provide it with copies of their church directories for use in get-out-the-vote efforts met with a rebuke from ten theologians who wrote to express their concern that the campaign was trying to engage churches in partisan politics. Others were unnerved by wire service reports that the president had asked a high-ranking Vatican official to "push the

American Catholic bishops to be more aggressive politically on family and life issues." America's religious institutions have long played a constructive role in promoting certain values in our society, and many politicians have long sought to find common cause in advancing such goals. Tactics such as these, however, go too far; they blur the distinction between the proper role of religion in government's business and of politics in religion's business.

Although they are often called conservatives, I believe the social fundamentalists have misappropriated the conservative banner. The defining feature of the conservative viewpoint is a faith in the ability, and a respect for the right, of individuals to make their own decisions—economic, social, and spiritual—about their lives. The true conservative understands that government's track record in respecting individual rights is poor when it dictates individual choices. Accordingly, the conservative desires to limit government's reach as much as possible. Traditional conservatives adhere to the maxim, often attributed to Thomas Jefferson, that government governs best that governs least. The social fundamentalists, on the other hand, are pushing to use government's power—and extend its influence—into even the most private aspects of people's lives in an effort to impose their views on everyone. Much of their agenda is simply inconsistent with true conservatism. They seem to have forgotten that one of America's greatest strengths has always been its ability to respect a broad range of ideas centered on a core set of values—freedom, opportunity, diversity. They also seem to have forgotten that you can respect specific differences while adhering to shared central principles.

The rise of the so-called religious right in American politics is certainly a product of the social upheaval that rocked the United States in the 1960s and 1970s. As America's social fabric seemed to unravel, virtually all of our social, cultural, and political institutions came under assault. To millions of Americans (people whom Richard Nixon famously called the Silent Majority), America seemed to be coming apart at the seams and something had to be done to restore the traditional values that had long been the norm in American life.

A number of groups were founded in the late 1970s in response to the cultural crisis that many saw America confronting. Paul Weyrich's Free Congress Research and Education Foundation, which started up in 1977, and Focus on the Family, founded by James Dobson in 1978 were just two. The one that quickly became the most prominent was Jerry Falwell's Moral Majority, established in 1979. The speed with which these groups (especially Falwell's) began to affect American political life prompted others to launch similar groups, including the Family Research Council, founded in 1983, and later, the Christian Coalition, which Pat Robertson established in 1989 following his unsuccessful run for the Republican presidential nomination in 1988. As they grew in size, they also grew in influence, not just in the private sphere but in the political system as well. Flush with their newfound power, this latest breed of religious leaders, mostly from the South, were no longer content to save souls one by one through the work of their churches. They set their sights higher, with their self-described mission being to save the nation's soul through its political institutions, using civil law to impose religious law. Jerry Falwell captured their goal when he proclaimed, "I have a Divine Mandate to go into the halls of Congress and fight for laws that will save America."

By 1992, when the first President Bush was seeking reelection, the social fundamentalists held (or, at least, were perceived to hold) an electoral veto over his success. When Bush lost, the conventional wisdom (especially among these groups) held that his defeat resulted from his inability to motivate the "conservative" base of the party. It appeared as if Robertson might be well on the way to achieving a goal he had laid out to the *Denver Post* just ten days before the election. "We want," he said, "as soon as possible to see a majority of the Republican Party in the hands of pro-family Christians by 1996."

Of all the social issues the social fundamentalists have pursued over the years, outlawing abortion has been the most ardent of their missions. This effort, and the extreme rhetoric—and even violence—that have been employed in its service, has crossed the lines of basic respect for the views and personal freedoms of others. For millions of Americans, on both sides of this issue, their pro-life or pro-choice position represents a deeply held and principled belief. However, I regret that too many in the leadership of both sides have decided they do not want to even attempt to find common ground with people holding the opposite view. Unfortunately, when principled stands become rigid stances, it is almost impossible to work constructively together, even on issues where agreement is possible.

Since the Supreme Court handed down its abortion ruling in 1973, only one pro-choice Republican has found a place on the GOP's presidential ticket: Gerald Ford, and he barely survived a primary challenge from Ronald Reagan. Every subsequent presidential and vice-presidential nominee—Reagan, George H. W. Bush, Dan Quayle, Bob Dole, Jack Kemp, George W. Bush, and Dick Cheney—supported efforts to overturn *Roe v. Wade* at the time they were nominated. Curiously, though, none of our successful standard-bearers made their abortion stances centerpieces of their campaigns and, until recently, abortion issues occupied a backseat to other domestic concerns of their administrations. Ronald Reagan, for example, never once appeared at the annual pro-life rally protesting the anniversary of *Roe v. Wade* in Washington. He always addressed the group by telephone— even when the participants were just across the street from the White House.

Nevertheless, for nearly thirty years now, no pro-choice Republican has broken the lock the antiabortion faction of the party has on the nominating process. The closest anyone ever came was George H. W. Bush, who changed his pro-choice stance to become an acceptable running mate for Ronald Reagan. On this issue, religious conservatives and others in the pro-life camp have had a death grip on the GOP. Yet despite their success in imposing abortion as a litmus test on Republican candidates, they have made no progress in persuading the American people of the need to outlaw abortion. According to the Gallup Poll, in 1975, 21 percent of Americans believed abortion should be legal under any circumstances, 54 percent believed it should be legal only under certain circumstances, and 22 percent believed it should be illegal in all circumstances. Today, after thirty years of debate, the numbers are virtually unchanged: 24 percent believe abortion should be legal under any circumstances, 55 percent believe it should be legal only under certain circumstances, and 19 percent believe it should be illegal in all circumstances. Remarkably little movement after so much time and so much rhetoric.

As I look back on my political career to date, I think it could be fairly said that I did not recognize early enough the rise of the social fundamentalists as a separate movement within the party. I first ran into them head-on on the abortion issue, and their vehemence, frankly, caught me by surprise. I had made the mistake of thinking social fundamentalists were primarily conservatives, and, as a result, I felt sure that my strong conservative record on so many issues would outweigh my pro-choice position in their calculation. That turned out to be true in my first campaign for governor in 1993.

In that campaign, the social fundamentalists had not yet gained much influence in the New Jersey Republican Party. Their movement, which had started in the South and West, had not yet reached the party in New Jersey in any significant way. I was running against the incumbent in the middle of New Jersey's deepest recession since the Great Depression, and my campaign naturally focused on what I would do to help jump-start my state's anemic economy. The centerpiece of my platform was my promise to cut New Jersey's income tax by 30 percent—a pledge right out of the conservative playbook.

The abortion issue received relatively little attention in both the primary and the general election campaigns, probably because all of my opponents in both races were pro-choice (even the so-called conservative in the GOP primary). What's perhaps most telling is the fact that the social fundamentalists were not yet organized enough to run a pro-life candidate in 1993. I did meet with pro-life leaders during the campaign, and they shared with me gruesome photographs of aborted fetuses and lectured me about the evil of my position. Because they were more interested at that point in defeating my opponent, they did not make any real effort to derail my campaign.

After I was elected, I kept my promise to cut taxes, and I also enacted a series of policies with strong appeal to conservatives. We controlled the growth of government spending, instituted tort reform and tough anticrime laws, and reformed welfare, enabling more than half of the recipients to move off the rolls. I felt confident that these achievements would win me the continuing support of conservatives. That belief was confirmed by attention from the party at the national level that our record began to attract. In 1995, at the start of just my second year as governor, I was chosen by Newt Gingrich, the first Republican Speaker of the House in forty years, to deliver the Republican response to President Clinton's State of the Union Address—becoming the first governor ever given that honor by either party. That was the year that the Contract with America led to Republican control of the Congress for the first time since Eisenhower's first term. Gingrich was getting most of the credit (deservedly so), and I saw his decision to ask me to deliver the Republican response at such a pivotal moment in our party's history as a sign that, despite his reputation as an unyielding conservative, he recognized that to make the GOP a truly national majority party, moderates had to be part of the equation.

Invitations also began to come into my office from Republican candidates all around the country who wanted me to campaign for them. I traveled extensively, raising money and stumping for Republicans across the party spectrum, ranging from conservatives like Rick Santorum of Pennsylvania to moderates like Linda Lingle in Hawaii.

Now it appears ironic that I was probably invited to campaign for more conservative candidates—many of them pro-life—than moderates. Back then—what now seems like ages ago—it seemed like common sense. In many parts of America, some Republican conservatives had apparently felt that campaigning with me and other moderates like me after they'd won their primaries could help soften their image with the broader electorate, whose votes they needed to win in the fall. Later on, during my own reelection campaign, I was disappointed when some (but not all) of the conservatives I had campaigned for declined to campaign for me.

My increased visibility, however, seemed to inflame and energize the social fundamentalists. They saw my popularity on the campaign trail as a threat to their growing crusade to remake the Republican Party in their own image. If a pro-choice Republican could demonstrate that she or he could work with pro-life conservatives (as evidenced by the several pro-life members of my senior staff), that would weaken their hold on their candidates. They clearly determined that this was a problem they were going to have to deal with firmly and decisively.

I first got a taste of what was to come when I was the cochair (along with Texas governor George W. Bush) of the 1996 Republican National Convention. I was slated to deliver a four-minute speech on the convention's second night. Mine, like most of the dozens of speeches that are delivered during a convention, wasn't particularly memorable—and it wasn't meant to be. The only speech people outside the convention hall are supposed to remember is the presidential candidate's acceptance speech.

That's why I was annoyed when the convention planners put up a huge fight with my staff over one line at the beginning of my remarks: "For all our differences, whether over the issue of choice or gun control, our Party is united by this goal: electing Bob Dole the President of the United States." This simple declarative statement was hardly earth-shattering, yet you would think I was calling for state-sponsored infanticide, the way the convention planners were reacting.

This battle was becoming distracting, so in the end, my staff and I agreed to delete the offending sentence from the text. When I took the podium to deliver my remarks, no mention of choice scrolled by on the TelePrompTer, but I ad-libbed the line back in. Of course, this did not please the convention planners, and some of those in the hall actually stood up and turned their backs on me as I continued. I had reinserted the line because I thought that it would be a sad day for the Republican Party if we couldn't even mention the fact that we had differences and because it was important to me to make that point. I didn't think we should repeat the error the Democrats made in 1992 when they had denied then Pennsylvania governor Bob Casey the opportunity to make a brief speech on abortion at their convention because he was pro-life.

After the convention, and with my own reelection coming up the following year, I became the recipient of an ever-growing chorus of advice about what I should do about my "abortion problem."

Political consultants of every stripe began to drop hints that if I ever wanted to be a viable national candidate in the Republican Party, I needed to start to think about how to moderate my pro-choice position. It was time, they counseled, to start laying the groundwork for what would be my eventual "epiphany," when I would declare that I had modified my pro-choice position to make it more acceptable to pro-life voters. They saw this strategy as an easy fix for my "abortion problem." I saw it as less than honest (and so did most of my advisers), and I wasn't about to change my beliefs.

I frankly find the so-called debate about abortion counterproductive and the tactics of the social fundamentalists offensive. I don't know anyone who is proabortion. Every person I've ever known or worked with who supports the right of the woman to make the choice about whether or not to continue a pregnancy has wished that no one ever had to confront that choice. I consider myself to be pro-life, but I also understand that there are times when a woman may face that terrible decision. I believe the truly conservative view is that it is a woman's choice to make for herself, not government's to dictate. The suggestion by some in the antiabortion movement that most women who undergo the trauma of an abortion are simply indulging themselves in a form of cosmetic surgery or birth control is insulting to all women. Even though there are some women who abuse their freedom of choice, they are in the distinct minority. Most Americans see this just the way I do; they're neither proabortion nor antichoice, but are somewhere in the middle.

Unfortunately, the extremes on both sides are defining the terms of the debate, and on both sides they are imposing such an ideologically pure litmus test that candidates and officeholders are distracted from pursuing policies that could prevent unwanted pregnancies or promote adoption. More than three decades after *Roe v. Wade,* this issue remains as supercharged and divisive today as it ever was.

A classic example of how such zealous ideological purity can stop the passage of effective policy was the battle I faced in New Jersey over the procedure known as partial-birth abortion. In this case, the antiabortion hard-liners in Trenton were so extreme that they undermined what would have been the passage of the first constitutionally sound restriction on late-term abortions in the country.

Prior to the mid-1990s, few people had ever heard of a partial-birth abortion, a medical procedure doctors call intact dilation and extraction. The procedure was developed only in the late 1980s as an alternative method of ending late-stage pregnancies. Rarely used, it is an admittedly horrific procedure, which, in my view, should be performed only when the physical health or life of the pregnant woman is at clear risk.

Pro-life leaders saw the development and practice of the partial-birth-abortion procedure as a powerfully persuasive tool in their effort to outlaw all abortions. Consequently, they launched what was a very effective effort to pass a national ban on partial-birth abortions, bringing this issue to the forefront of the abortion debate and using graphic descriptions to make their point that this was a horrendous way to end a pregnancy. They were so successful that in 1996, Congress sent a bill outlawing partial-birth abortions to President Clinton's desk. The vote in the House of Representatives was overwhelming, with more than enough members in favor of the bill to override an expected presidential veto. The vote in the Senate, however, was nowhere near the two thirds that would have been needed for an override. Citing the bill's failure to provide an exception to protect the health of the mother, President Clinton vetoed it.

Coming, as it did, in a presidential election year, Clinton's veto unleashed a torrent of criticism from most Republicans. Bob Dole, the soon-to-be Republican presidential nominee, said that Clinton's veto "put him out on the extremist fringe" of the pro-choice crowd, while Republican social fundamentalists such as Gary Bauer predicted that Clinton's veto would "haunt him" at the polls.

The day after the veto, I held one of my regular public events at the statehouse in Trenton, a forum I often used to make announcements and answer questions from the media. Following the announcement (on an issue totally unrelated to abortion), I opened the floor to the press. Not surprisingly, it wasn't long before I was asked for my reaction to the president's veto of the partial-birth-abortion bill, and I answered, "I believe the president was right." Needless to say, that answer—and the further explanation I proceeded to offer about why I thought the veto was appropriate—provoked an immediate outcry from the social fundamentalists.

Although I was not the only Republican to support the veto, there weren't very many of us. Two weeks later, *National Review* said that those Republicans who supported the veto had "shown that they are the spokesmen not for a major wing of the GOP, but for an extremist fringe." Yet polls taken in 1996 showed that only a bare majority of 54 percent of Republican primary voters favored keeping the Party's platform plank calling for a constitutional ban on abortion. That hardly put me in an extremist fringe.

This is a perfect illustration of just how complicated the abortion issue really is. As soon as the controversy erupted, I realized that I should have articulated my position in a way that more fully reflected my thinking. My primary concern about that particular bill was that it failed to make an exception that protected both the physical health and the life of the mother. Most Americans do not believe that an unborn child has a greater right to life than does the mother carrying that child. Indeed, a CNN/Time/Gallup Poll taken in 2003 showed that overwhelming majorities favor the right of a woman to have an abortion if her life or physical health is seriously threatened by continuing a pregnancy. Explaining my position in those terms might have softened the response of the social fundamentalists. That being said, however, I don't believe it actually would have deterred them from using the issue to attempt to marginalize me in the Republican Party, as they soon tried to do.

Because the president had vetoed the national bill, and the Congress was unable to override his veto, the issue quickly made its way to the states. Within months, more than a dozen states had passed partial-birth-abortion bans, and in New Jersey, despite the state's long-standing support for a woman's right to choose, the social fundamentalists saw an opening. Not only was I up for re-election myself, but so was the entire state assembly and the state senate. The state's pro-life lobby threatened to use their leverage to oppose in the primaries any candidate who did not favor a total ban on partial-birth abortions, no matter what that person's positions were on all the other issues. In response, the Republican

Speaker of the state assembly made the passage of a total partial-birth-abortion ban (without any exceptions) one of his top legislative priorities for 1997.

I felt that was a mistake. The Republican Party had a great record to run on that year, and we didn't need the distraction— and the division—that this issue would cause. Both my senior staff and I worked hard to persuade the Speaker to hold off. I remember telling him, in effect, "You don't want to do this; it's bad politics, bad policy, and it's unconstitutional besides. I'll have no choice but to veto it." He refused to reconsider.

On May 8, 1997, the state assembly passed a bill banning so-called partial-birth abortions, ignoring my efforts to persuade them to include an exception for the life and physical health of the mother. They knew as well as I did how hardened the social fundamentalists' position was, and that providing such an exception would just draw their ire and their political fire. Understandably, they didn't want to face that. Yet because the bill failed to provide the protection for women, I stated very clearly that I could not sign it if it came to my desk. "I am very concerned," I said, "that so far the legislation has no provision that considers the health of the mother and I think that's critical. I simply can't ignore the health of the mother. I simply can't."

The legislative leaders were not happy. They knew they had put me in a tough spot, but they were also in a difficult position: their bill failed to sufficiently protect a woman's health, and it was clearly unconstitutional. The lawyers who worked for me told them that, and so did their own lawyers. They were clearly so intimidated by the social fundamentalist activists, however, that they cared more about satisfying that minority faction's extremist demands than they did about passing a bill that would actually become law.

In the days that followed, I came under intense pressure to change my position, as many other Republicans were already doing. The most prominent call came from the *Wall Street Journal*, whose Washington columnist took me to task for not changing my mind, lecturing me in the headline of the piece that it was A GOOD WAY NOT TO RUN FOR PRESIDENT and branding me as the "last prominent extremist" in the Republican Party who "so relish[ed] sticking a thumb in the eye of social conservatives that [she'd] endorse later-term abortions."

I found the *Journal*'s arguments out of character. Its editorial page had long prided itself on advocating positions based on principle, not politics. To be told that I should change my principles because it would be politically expedient was, I thought, inconsistent. I decided to respond in a letter to the editor—a tactic I rarely used because, as they say, it's best not to get into an argument with someone who buys ink by the barrel.

"Over the course of my public career," I wrote, "I have opposed efforts to expand the scope of government's reach into people's everyday lives as a matter of policy. I believe that the deeply personal choice to terminate or continue a pregnancy belongs to a woman, her doctor, and her religious adviser. I do not believe that public officials have the right to inject their own beliefs into this profoundly personal decision." I went on to explain, "I do believe that government has an obligation to protect those who are unable to protect themselves. I would sign legislation that came to me saying that, past a certain point in a pregnancy, abortion is not an option—except to protect the life or health of the mother.

I could support language that would ensure that 'health' refers only to situations where there is a significant risk of serious physical injury or impairment to the mother. A pregnant woman is also a human being, whose life and health also deserve consideration."

To its credit, the *Journal* ran my letter in full, and on the same day it also printed one from the president of the Republican Coalition for Choice, Susan Cullman. In her letter, she related the results of a recent national poll that had showed that more than eight out of ten respondents agreed with the statement: "The decision to have the abortion procedure known as the so-called 'partial birth procedure or late-term abortions' is a medical decision that should be made by a woman, her doctor, her family, and her clergy." I couldn't have said it better myself.

The most important point of this story is that although I opposed that specific version of the bill, I had said I was willing to sign a bill that banned any abortion past a certain point in a pregnancy as long as the physical health and life of the mother could be protected. The irony is that New Jersey remains one of the few states with virtually unregulated abortions. I had provided the path to the enactment of a constitutionally sound regulation of late-term abortions, but the social fundamentalist political operatives and their allies in Trenton refused to follow it. Frankly, it seemed to me at the time (and still does today) that their failure to take the path I had laid out suggested that they were more interested in having an issue than in saving the lives of unborn children.

When the legislature went right ahead and passed an unconstitutional version of the bill, I used the New Jersey governor's unique power of conditional veto to rewrite it and sent it back to the legislature with my proposed language to protect the physical health of the mother. They decided not to take any further action until after the election, and so from that day through Election Day, the social fundamentalists took advantage of every opportunity to brand me as the abortion extremist who wouldn't even put an end to what she herself had called a "horrific way to end a pregnancy." At virtually every campaign stop I made that fall, I was greeted by protesters labeling me a baby killer, and the jabs didn't stop at the New Jersey border.

Chicago Sun-Times columnist Robert Novak wrote several columns excoriating me. The *National Review* ran a profile that called me "a symbol of country-club social liberalism" who is "hostile to conservatives and in favor of big government and radical social policy." The *Washington Post* quoted one self-identified New Jersey Republican who wanted me defeated as saying, "She's dangerous because she is articulate [and] like a stealth bomber. A Whitman victory would be a setback to the Republican Party." As one New Jersey columnist wrote near the end of the campaign, "The contest among conservatives to deliver the unkindest cut of all in what appears to be a concerted effort to consign Christine Todd Whitman to the ash heap of history has been fierce." Even the international press took notice. The day before Election Day, the *Times* of London, under the headline CHRISTIAN RIGHT TAKES SHINE OFF REPUBLICAN GOLDEN GIRL, wrote, "Ms. Whitman finds herself damned for championing policies that used to be in the party's mainstream but are now seen as 'too liberal.'" As far as I was concerned, the London *Times* got it exactly right. The attacks on me served notice—as they were intended to—to moderate

Republicans around the rest of the country about what would happen to them if they didn't toe the line on this issue.

I was angry and frustrated that the issue had found a place in the campaign. After all, the last thing any candidate running for reelection wants is to be put on the defensive on a controversial issue. I had hoped to run on what I felt was a positive, impressive record during my first term—fulfilling my promise to cut the state income tax by 30 percent (and doing so a year ahead of schedule), stimulating a record pace of job creation, passing tough anticrime legislation, enacting meaningful welfare reform, improving the condition of New Jersey's environment. My Republican colleagues in the legislature and I shared this list of achievements, and they should have had the conviction that we had a strong enough record that we didn't need to bow to the social fundamentalists. I believe that the failure in recent years of Republican candidates to stand up to such pressure and take a more reasonable stance on abortion rights—a position polls consistently show the majority of the American people clearly prefers—has only dug the party deeper and deeper into a hole on this issue. Ironically, those who seem to have understood this danger most clearly at the time were some of the traditional conservatives in the party.

Lyn Nofziger, a Goldwater Republican who had helped manage all three of Ronald Reagan's presidential campaigns and had served as Reagan's White House political director, dropped everything to come to New Jersey to provide me with expert advice and counsel. Rick Santorum, a strong conservative, took a lot of flak from the social fundamentalist wing of the party for coming in to campaign for me, as did Dan Quayle. Although none of these people agreed with me on choice (in fact, someone told me recently about seeing Lyn in the spring of 2004, when Lyn had said, "I think Christie Whitman's great, even if she is wrong on all the issues"), they could see beyond this one issue.

I managed to hold on and win reelection—but by a much closer margin than I had hoped. The party also retained control of both houses of the legislature, but the episode took its toll. It detracted from my ability, as the head of the ticket, to promote our strong record of accomplishment, and in the end, accomplished nothing. After the election, both houses of the legislature overrode my veto—the first and only override of my governorship—and sure enough, just as the legal experts had advised, within short order a suit was filed challenging the bill's constitutionality. The state legislature spent more than half a million of the taxpayers' dollars defending the bill, even though the legislature's own lawyers had said the case was unwinnable. In July 2000, the United States Court of Appeals for the Third Circuit found the law unconstitutional and voided it. A panel of that court subsequently ordered the legislature to pay the legal costs incurred by pro-choice groups in challenging the law.

Three years later, I received confirmation from an unlikely source that the social conservatives had never even listened to my arguments back in 1997. In 2000, I briefly considered running for an open U.S. Senate seat in New Jersey. As part of my early effort to take the political temperature, I called a number of influential Republicans to get their reaction to my candidacy. One of them was the Reverend Pat Robertson. He wanted to know about the partial-birth abortion controversy in New Jersey, so I laid it all out for him. When I finished, he paused only a second before telling me, "I could support that."

Although we were able to win in 1997, despite the efforts of the social fundamentalists, they did a good deal more damage in future years to the party in New Jersey. They were unable to unseat me that year, but their control of the party did remove the Republicans from power in Trenton, four years later. In 2001, with the strong backing of the social fundamentalists, the Republicans nominated Bret Schundler, the former mayor of Jersey City, for governor. Schundler had defeated Congressman Bob Franks, a pro-choice Republican, in the primary—this despite the fact that Franks had a proven record of being able to attract votes statewide. (Just the year before, Franks had come within a whisker of winning a seat in the U.S. Senate, losing to Jon Corzine, a multimillionaire Democrat who spent more than sixty million dollars of his own money on the campaign.) Not only did Schundler lose in a landslide to the Democrats, but the Republicans also lost control of both houses of the legislature. I have no doubt that had Franks been nominated, we would not have suffered the huge losses we did, and we might even have won.

Today, the social fundamentalists in New Jersey may control the party's nominating process statewide, but the Republicans don't control anything in the state government. The social fundamentalists have made little headway in terms of changing national abortion policy, although they have alienated many voters—especially women. Far from being resolved, this seemingly irresolvable debate has now carried over into another highly contentious fight: stem cell research.

After Ronald Reagan announced to the nation that he had Alzheimer's disease and would be withdrawing from public life, the previously obscure issue of stem cell research began to get national attention, and has now become yet another social fundamentalist wedge issue. A measure of how deep the divide is over this issue is the fact that it is pitting the social fundamentalists against a conservative icon: Nancy Reagan. Her support for removing restrictions on the use of federal research funds for stem cell research has made her, in the words of her daughter, Patti, "a central figure in the effort to get the federal government out of the way" on stem cell research. Yet even their respect for Ronald Reagan wasn't enough to keep some of the leading voices of the social fundamentalist wing of the GOP from dismissing, just days after her husband's death, Nancy Reagan's advocacy for stem cell research, some quite condescendingly so.

Using much the same tactic others employed against Goldwater in his later years, Dr. James Dobson, of Focus on the Family, said that "politicians and the media are using this grieving widow to unwittingly confuse the general public," and Ann Coulter wrote, "Someone persuaded poor, dear Nancy Reagan that research on human embryos might have saved her Ronnie from Alzheimer's. Now the rest of us are supposed to shut up because the wife of America's greatest President (oh, save your breath, girls!) supports stem cell research." Even Michael Reagan dismissed his stepmother's views by asserting that Nancy has been "allowed to believe" that stem cell research holds promise. I can only imagine how Ronald Reagan would have reacted to such attacks on his wife from people who claim to have respected and admired him.

Nancy Reagan understands, in ways the social fundamentalists don't seem to quite fully comprehend, that showing concern for life should also extend to the living. Human embryonic stem cells are thought by scientists to hold enormous potential for finding cures for such devastating diseases as Parkinson's and Lou Gehrig's, various types of cancer and diabetes, spinal cord injuries, and, just maybe, Alzheimer's. The social fundamentalists oppose such research, however, because the stem cells that hold the most promise can be acquired only from human embryos; and they apparently believe that cells from an embryo that may be just a few days old—and contains just a few cells—are the equivalent of a third-trimester fetus. The pro-life slogan, "Abortion stops a beating heart," doesn't apply in this case.

Certainly precautions must be taken to try to prevent the irresponsible exploitation of this research, but that is a challenge we face every day with a host of new technologies and information. No responsible scientist is suggesting the deliberate creation of human embryos for the sole purpose of harvesting stem cells. Not only would that be unethical, it's also unnecessary. Thousands of embryos, created through in vitro fertilization, sit frozen and abandoned in countless fertility clinics in every corner of America. It is possible that such embryos could, under proper regulation and supervision, be used to develop the stem cell lines that could cure diseases that afflict millions. It's at least worth talking about. How can we let the extreme extension of a rigid ideology forestall an honest discussion about how we might, ethically and responsibly, advance research that could benefit literally millions of people in the United States and around the world?

Unfortunately, however, too many Republicans have used support for embryonic stem cell research as a cudgel with which to attack other Republicans. In the 2004 Florida senate primary, my former cabinet colleague Mel Martinez ran an attack ad against his opponent Bill McCollum (a former congressman who had frequently earned 100 percent ratings from the National Right to Life Committee for his voting record in Congress) for supporting such research. McCollum had said, "I'm pro-life, but I also believe that a critical part of being pro-life is helping the living."

It was a campaign ad so offensive in its tone that even Florida Governor Jeb Bush called Martinez to ask him to take it off the air. Martinez came from behind and won the primary, but not before losing the endorsement of the *St. Petersburg Times*, which said it did not want to be "associated with bigotry" and retracted its endorsement of Martinez in favor of McCollum, as well as losing the respect of many of his fellow Republicans. If the 2004 election was truly an affirmation of support for the social fundamentalist agenda, this race would refute that. President Bush carried Florida by a comfortable 5-point margin while Mel Martinez won his new Senate seat by a razor-thin 1 percentage point.

The issue of abstinence as the only aspect of sex education for adolescents is another example of where social fundamentalists are out of step with traditional conservative thought. Most people agree that promoting abstinence is an important part of any sex education program. After all, the only sure way—100 percent guaranteed—to prevent an unwanted pregnancy or avoid contracting a sexually transmitted disease is through abstinence. As governor, I supported and funded efforts to introduce abstinence education into New Jersey's schools as part of a comprehensive sex education program. Experience has shown, however, that kids need to be taught about other ways they can protect themselves against pregnancy and STDs. Too often, teenagers' sincere vows to remain abstinent come in conflict with their hormones. One recent study showed that 60 percent of college students who had taken abstinence vows in high school or middle school had broken that vow; another national study showed that those who had taken a pledge to remain abstinent were more likely to have unprotected sex if they broke their pledge.

Social fundamentalists vociferously argue that abstinence-only education is the only acceptable approach and that if birth control is mentioned at all, it should be in the context of its failure. They are certainly entitled to that view and to promote it. Where they diverge from traditional conservatism, however, is in their insistence that the federal government control how individual school districts teach sex ed. If being conservative means limiting the reach of government, forcing thousands of school districts to teach sex ed in a certain way is certainly inconsistent with traditional conservatism. It's also basically wrongheaded.

In our driver education classes, we teach teenagers not to speed or drive recklessly. But because we understand the risks on the highway, we also teach them to use their seat belts. We should be doing the same thing when it comes to sex education—urging them to remain abstinent until marriage, but equipping them with the information they need to be safe. That strikes me as both reasonable and responsible.

Apparently, President Bush came to the same conclusion. In June 2004, in a speech about HIV/AIDS prevention at the Greater Exodus Baptist Church in Philadelphia, the president recommended what's known as the A-B-C approach to preventing the spread of HIV. As he explained it, A-B-C stands for

"Abstain, be faithful in marriage, and when appropriate, use condoms." He went on to say this is a "practical, balanced, and moral message," and pointed to the success nations like Uganda (a country not otherwise known for progressive social policy) have had in using this message to prevent the spread of HIV. The president's statement should help prevent a repeat of the reception that Tommy Thompson, the secretary of Health and Human Services, received at an international AIDS conference in Spain in 2002, when he was basically booed out of the room.

Bush's remarks echoed those made by Secretary of State Colin Powell two years earlier during an appearance on MTV. "In my own judgment, condoms are a way to prevent infection," Powell said, "and therefore I not only support their use, I encourage their use among people who are sexually active and need to protect themselves." Social fundamentalists exploded in outrage at Powell's message. The head of the Family Research Council called Powell's statement "reckless and irresponsible," and the president of Concerned Women for America declared that the Secretary of State had "undercut the moral authority of all parents [and] embarrassed President Bush." Interestingly, Focus on the Family even suggested that Powell needed to familiarize himself with the HIV/AIDS prevention policies of Uganda—the very country President Bush two years later held up as an example of how a balanced approach to sexually transmitted disease prevention can succeed.

The latest high-octane issue on the social fundamentalist agenda is gay marriage. How many people realize, I wonder, that their support for a constitutional amendment to prohibit gay marriages, if successful, would result in only the second time the

Constitution had been amended to *restrict* freedom, the first having been the nation's failed effort at Prohibition? The federal government has never been in the business of regulating marriage or issuing marriage licenses. That has always been left up to the states, which write the laws governing marriage and issue marriage licenses, and if there ever were an issue where the Republican Party ought to be traditionally federalist—meaning against intrusive federal regulation—this is it. The 2004 election cycle showed that the states are perfectly able to address this issue without the need for a federal constitutional amendment. Eleven states had various proposals on the ballot to ban gay marriages (and in many cases civil unions and domestic partner arrangements). The citizens of those states got the opportunity to be heard on the issue. In addition, there is a federal law on the books that explicitly preserves the rights of states to recognize whatever forms of marriage they choose. It's called the Defense of Marriage Act, and it was passed by a Republican Congress and signed into law by President Clinton in 1996. So as recently as 1996, the official Republican position was the solidly conservative one: let the people of each state decide whether or not to allow homosexuals to marry in their state. If a state decides to permit such unions, so be it. Similarly, if states decide to prohibit such unions (as nearly forty have), their authority should also be respected. I think Dick Cheney expressed it best during the 2000 campaign, which he reiterated in 2004: "I think the fact of the matter, of course, is that the matter is regulated by the states. . . . I don't think there should be a federal policy in this area."

Although polls suggest that a clear majority of the American people oppose gay marriage, they also show that people are almost evenly divided on amending the Constitution to prohibit it. That is, of course, far below the level of support needed to ratify an amendment (two thirds of the House and Senate and three quarters of the states). Regardless of what polls show, it is unfortunate that the leaders of the social fundamentalist wing of the party haven't followed President Bush's request to conduct the debate without "bitterness or anger."

Instead, they have framed the debate as a crusade against "perversion," an effort to forestall the United States from becoming "the fountainhead of filth and immorality" in the world, and a battle to prevent the inevitable legalization of polygamy and incest that would follow if gay marriage or civil unions were permitted. In response to the argument that a homosexual couple's private relationship isn't a threat to traditional marriage, one Republican senator, John Cornyn of Texas, went so far as to say, "It does not affect your daily life very much if your neighbor marries a box turtle. But that does not mean it is right. . . . Now you must raise your children up in a world where that union of a man and a box turtle is on the same legal footing as man and wife." I guess we should at least be grateful he didn't use a snapping turtle in his example.

Republicans of every stripe should be denouncing such alarmist talk. Because we don't, we are tarred by the same brush—seen as intolerant and narrow-minded by the millions of moderates who may not support gay marriage but who nevertheless are against ostracizing or persecuting homosexuals.

That failure may be what helped prompt the 2004 Republican platform committee to insert language that acknowledges that "members of our Party can have deeply held and sometimes differing views" and that "this diversity is a source of strength, not a sign of weakness." While that may not sound like much, it represents a vast shift from the days, back at the 1996 Republican convention, when I was censored for even trying to acknowledge that there were differences within the party.

It's interesting that with this issue we are seeing what may be the first cracks in the uneasy alliances many traditional conservatives have made with the social fundamentalists. Many prominent conservatives, both in and out of government, are opposed to a constitutional amendment to ban same-sex marriages. In addition to the vice president and Lynne Cheney, they include former Congressman Bob Barr of Georgia (the sponsor of the Defense of Marriage Act and one of the leaders in the Clinton impeachment drive), Congressman Jim Sensenbrenner, chairman of the House Judiciary Committee, columnist George Will, and even Ann Coulter.

The conservative columnist David Brooks had an interesting take on the entire issue, writing in the *New York Times* in support of gay marriage. He argued, "The conservative course is not to banish gay people from making such commitments. It is to *expect* that they make such commitments. We shouldn't just allow gay marriage. We should *insist* on gay marriage. We should regard it as scandalous that two people could claim to love each other and not want to sanctify their love with marriage and fidelity."

When President Bush decided to endorse the ban, I immediately thought of the gays and lesbians I had worked with closely throughout my political career, many of whom were in long-term committed relationships and who also happened to be hardworking loyal Republicans. These gay Republicans had worked hard for the president's election in 2000, and several had also served with distinction as political appointees in the Reagan and Bush administrations. They had served the party loyally and their fellow citizens with dedication. The president's announcement must have come as a deep disappointment, as, once again, the social fundamentalists succeeded in driving a wedge between Republicans.

Ronald Reagan once said, "You do not get to be a majority party by searching for groups you won't associate or work with." That is even truer when those people are already in your party. So while the GOP succeeded in achieving majority party status with the 2004 elections, it will have a difficult, if not impossible, time maintaining that position if it ends up driving moderates out of the party.

Moderate Republicans such as Rudolph Giuliani and Arnold Schwarzenegger have clearly demonstrated that they can attract and hold the support of the traditional Republican base while expanding the party's appeal to moderate Democrats and independents. And although much has been made over the past four years about the stark division of the country into red and blue states on the national level, moderate Republicans have shown they can win even in the blue states. Of the twenty states that President Bush lost in the 2000 election, fifteen either had then, or have since elected, a moderate Republican governor. This suggests that if the Republican Party at the national level did a better job appealing to moderate voters in those states, instead of writing them off, the GOP could build a much stronger majority and thus help guide America out of extreme polarization and into a more unified future. The party can't do that, however, if it continues to embrace extremist positions on this set of our most divisive social issues.

CHAPTER FOUR

Reclaiming Lincoln's Legacy

There's no escaping the fact that the party of Lincoln has not always carried the mantle of Lincoln.

GEORGE W. BUSH, 2000

African American voters are the most loyal members of the Democratic Party's electoral coalition. In virtually any national, state, or local election, most Democratic candidates can generally count on receiving upwards of 90 percent of the African American vote—John Kerry received 89 percent in 2004. Bill Clinton had such success in connecting with the black community that in 1998 he was famously dubbed the "first black president" by Nobel Laureate Toni Morrison, a sentiment reaffirmed by the Congressional Black Caucus at its annual awards dinner in 2001 when the caucus chair echoed Morrison's well-known statement in her remarks and by the Arkansas Black Hall of Fame in 2003, when he became the first white person inducted into that body.

Yet for all Clinton's success in persuading black Americans that his administration was on their side, one of the first problems

I had to confront when I took over at the EPA was an enormous backlog in processing discrimination complaints filed by EPA employees against the agency itself. African Americans and other minorities who believed they were victims of discrimination at EPA were being forced to wait years to get the complaint hearing they deserved. Allegations of widespread discriminatory practices were being filed on a regular basis, yet not enough was being done to address the issues. Justice delayed is justice denied—and for hundreds of minority employees, the justice they sought was certainly being denied.

Just three months before I assumed my position at the EPA, the House Science Committee held a dramatic almost four-hour-long hearing to probe reports of discrimination at the agency and delays in addressing civil rights complaints. My predecessor, Carol Browner, testified, as did several African American EPA career employees who alleged that they were victims of discrimination. The head of the NAACP's Federal Sector Task Force put it this way: "Discrimination at the EPA is real, painful, and pervasive. . . . There seems to be a situation at EPA where if you complain or ask questions about what is wrong, you are facing a death sentence in terms of upward mobility and promotions."

During the preparation for my Senate confirmation hearings, I watched the videotape of those proceedings. The stories told were deeply disturbing, and the questioning from the committee was sharp. At one point, Carol Browner was reduced to tears. It was clear that the EPA had a serious civil rights problem. This should have been big national news. It's not often, after all, that a member of the president's cabinet breaks down in a congressional hearing, and it had to be news that the Clinton administration was itself being accused—from the inside—of ignoring discrimination against African Americans. Yet after a thorough search, I learned that there was virtually no coverage of the hearing. Aside from a short article buried deep in the front section of the *Washington Post*, and an article in an obscure weekly newsletter, the media had apparently ignored the story totally.

A few weeks later, at my confirmation hearing, I received only one question about the civil rights problem facing the EPA—and that was from a liberal Democrat, asking me to continue the policies of the Clinton administration, policies which had clearly failed. That was advice I did not take.

Instead, I made it an immediate priority to eliminate the backlog of complaints. To tackle this problem, I brought in the Reverend DeForest "Buster" Soaries, a black minister who had served as secretary of state in New Jersey in my second term as governor. In just four and a half months, Buster, my counselor Jessica Furey, and their team were able to reduce the number of backlogged discrimination cases filed by EPA employees by more than 90 percent. I also required every EPA supervisor and manager to attend a two-day national civil rights training program (I was one of the first to attend this course), and I issued every one of EPA's eighteen thousand employees a copy of the agency's Policy on Equal Employment Opportunity and Prohibiting Discrimination and Harassment.

Our efforts to undo the benign neglect of the eight previous years received almost as little attention as the problems themselves did. It seemed to me that the media was so convinced that Democrats could do no wrong on civil rights, and Republicans could do nothing right, that any news to the contrary wasn't worth covering—it was, at best, an aberration; at worst, just an insincere smokescreen.

The treatment that both aspects of this story received illustrates the challenge facing the Republican Party in seeking support from black voters. The Democrats have done such a good job of locking up the support of the black community that just about anything the Republican Party does in the interest of blacks is either ignored as an aberration or characterized as disingenuous. On the other hand, it must be said that the Republican Party's efforts to reach out to African American voters have been marred by clumsiness, a lack of consistent commitment, and an apparent tolerance for intolerance by too many Republican officeholders. When a national Republican leader wonders aloud, as Trent Lott did, about how much better the country would be today if Strom Thurmond, running in 1948 on the Dixiecrat ticket as a states' rights segregationist, had been elected president—and the leaders of the party fail to swiftly disassociate themselves from such sentiments because they don't want to undermine his position— it does more damage to the reputation of the Republican Party among minorities and moderates than the appointment of the first black secretary of state does to enhance it.

Hard as it is to believe today, when my parents were young, the GOP was the preferred party of African Americans and had as strong a claim on their votes as the Democrats do now. The Republican Party has long called itself the party of Lincoln—an expression of pride that the party was founded in support of personal freedoms, including freedom for African American slaves, and the proposition that all Americans deserve an equal opportunity to pursue the American dream. The motto of the party when it was founded in 1854 was "Free soil, free labor, free speech, free men." Lincoln signed the Emancipation Proclamation, but it was through the aggressive actions of the Republican Party after the war that the thirteenth, fourteenth, and fifteenth amendments to the Constitution—abolishing slavery, ensuring equal protection under the law to all Americans, and guaranteeing the voting rights of African Americans—were adopted. The great African American abolitionist Frederick Douglass once said that for black Americans, "The Republican Party is the ship and all else the sea."

In contrast, in the years leading up to the Civil War, Democratic Party leaders fought to protect slavery, and after the war they were a consistent impediment to every progressive effort made during Reconstruction. For a hundred years, the Democrats' close identification with policies preserving segregation, poll taxes and literacy tests, antimiscegenation laws, and all the other elements of what came to be known as Jim Crow kept the South solidly in the Democratic camp. Republicans in the 1920s were as confident of carrying the black vote as Democrats are today.

Yet for the past forty years, the Republican Party has utterly failed to earn the support of black voters. Where Douglass once hailed the Republican Party as a refuge, African Americans today too often see Republicans as hostile to their interests. Just ask J. C. Watts, a black Republican who served four terms in the House of Representatives in the 1990s. His own father once told him, "A black man voting Republican is like a chicken voting for Colonel Sanders." As complete as the abandonment of the GOP by black voters is today, it did not happen overnight.

Franklin Roosevelt was the first Democratic president to suc-

ceed in attracting significant support from African American voters. Coming into office in the midst of the Great Depression,
Roosevelt promised a New Deal for the needy and dispossessed in
America, and he struck a particular chord with black Americans,
who were still struggling to overcome the heavy burden of sys-
temic discrimination in the South. At the same time, their hopes
for a better life in northern cities were being crushed under the
weight of the terrible economic conditions afflicting the country.
Although Roosevelt was always careful not to do anything overt
to alienate the Solid South (perhaps remembering the political
turmoil his cousin Republican president Theodore Roosevelt had
unleashed when he invited Booker T. Washington to dinner at
the White House during his presidency thirty years before), there's
no doubt that black Americans saw him as a leader who was sympathetic to their situation.

Eleanor Roosevelt, however, was much more willing to ignore
the political ramifications that her husband had to contend with
as president and head of the Democratic Party. Although it's difficult to isolate any single event as the turning point in the shift
of black voters to the Democrats, one moving symbolic and principled act on her part certainly had a profound and lasting effect.
In 1939 she resigned her membership in the Daughters of the
American Revolution because they refused to allow Marian
Anderson, the internationally acclaimed African American singer,
to perform in their concert hall, located just a few hundred yards
from the White House. Mrs. Roosevelt then arranged for the concert to be held on the steps of the Lincoln Memorial on Easter
Sunday, despite the fact that she was well aware she'd anger southern Democrats. This simple, largely symbolic act allied her husband

and his party with the hopes and dreams of black Americans as never before. It helped turn the tide away from seventy years of African American support for the Republican Party.

Even though the tide had turned, it was another twenty years before it ran out on the GOP. Republican presidential candidates in the 1940s and 1950s continued to attract upward of 40 percent of the black vote. Despite the efforts of FDR and Harry Truman (who desegregated the armed forces after the conclusion of World War II), the Democratic Party remained deeply divided by racial politics. It was, after all, Democratic governors, Democratic state legislatures, and Democratic judges in the South who had erected Jim Crow and were fighting any and all efforts to dismantle it. All the way through the 1960 election, Republican presidential candidates still carried about 35 to 40 percent of black votes.

The almost complete exodus of black voters from the Republican Party didn't take place at the national level until 1964, when the GOP nominated Barry Goldwater, despite his vote against the Civil Rights Act of 1964. Goldwater received just 9 percent of the black vote in the general election, and since that election, Republican presidential candidates have had trouble earning much more than one of every ten votes cast by African Americans. Although the actual record of Republicans in the Congress, as well as in the state legislatures, does not support the contention that the party is against the interests of African Americans, it has not done an effective job of making that case.

In fact, the GOP has been a much stronger, more reliable supporter of civil rights initiatives and other matters of concern to the black community than many people appreciate. A Republican president, Dwight D. Eisenhower, established the U.S. Civil Rights

Commission. In 1966, the first black person ever elected to the U.S. Senate by popular vote, Edward Brooke of Massachusetts, was a Republican. When Richard Nixon took office in 1969, 68 percent of the black students in the South still attended segregated schools, despite the Supreme Court's *Brown v. Board of Education* decision fifteen years earlier. By 1974, because of the work of Nixon's Cabinet Committee on Education, chaired by George Shultz (later secretary of state under Ronald Reagan), just 8 percent of black students in the South were attending segregated schools. In addition, Nixon was the architect of the nation's first affirmative action plan, established to provide minority businesses greater contracting opportunities with the federal government. The only African American to join the Supreme Court in the past thirty-five years was appointed by a Republican, and the only major piece of civil rights legislation enacted into law in the past fifteen years was signed by the first President Bush.

Though many today seem to have forgotten, or have chosen not to remember, Republicans were indispensable in the battle for civil rights. Republicans played a key role in passing the landmark Civil Rights Act of 1964, still the single most important civil rights law ever enacted in America. This historic and long overdue measure would not have survived without the strong support of the Republican minority leader Everett Dirksen of Illinois. In fact, it took Dirksen and the Republican caucus to break a filibuster led by West Virginia Democratic Senator Robert Byrd—the longest filibuster in Senate history—enabling the bill to come to the floor for a vote. Only 61 percent of House Democrats and 69 percent of Senate Democrats voted for the bill versus 80 percent of Republicans in both houses.

Quite simply, had it not been for strong Republican support, southern Democrats would have prevented the Civil Rights Act of 1964 from becoming law. And although Democrats never tire of pointing out that Barry Goldwater voted against that bill, so, too, did such Senate Democrats as Albert Gore, Sr. (father of the former vice president), and J. William Fulbright (the man Bill Clinton called his political mentor). In fact, a study of the major civil rights votes taken in Congress since 1933, when black voters began to shift their allegiance from the Republicans to the Democrats, shows that a majority of Republicans favored civil rights in more than 96 percent of the votes, whereas a majority of Democrats opposed civil rights legislation in more than 80 percent of those same votes.

So how have the Republicans come to be seen as hostile to the hopes and aspirations of African Americans? This perception is a result of the party's overt and often ham-handed efforts, beginning with Barry Goldwater, to attract the support of white southern Democrats who were disaffected by the embrace of some in their party of the civil rights movement, beginning in the later part of the Kennedy administration and taking off under Lyndon Johnson. Because of the success of the GOP's so-called Southern Strategy, the Democrats' once Solid South has, over the past four decades, become prime Republican real estate, as the 2004 election clearly showed.

As the Republicans have solidified their base in the South, they have also solidified the resentment of African Americans nationwide. As southern Democrats came into the party through one door, African Americans left through another. We've come a long way in this country in matters of race relations since 1964, and there is wide middle ground on race issues today. Clearly, however, the Republican Party has not done an effective job in claiming that middle ground and advancing its efforts to win back the support of African Americans. In 2004, the Bush campaign did launch an effort to reach out to black clergy. Unfortunately, such efforts are too often the exception and are viewed by many as too little too late, coming only during the campaign season.

The conventional wisdom among many political operatives is that any effort by Republicans to win black votes is a waste of time, which creates a self-fulfilling prophecy. You don't have to have a political science Ph.D. to know that voters do not support candidates—or political parties—that ignore them. There are a great many Republicans who reject that notion, but their efforts to improve the party's reputation in the African American and other minority communities have not yet translated into significant levels of support.

The Republican Party's overall failure to successfully engage African American voters has allowed the Democrats to take the African American vote for granted. A number of prominent African American leaders have started to make this key point. During his run for the Democratic presidential nomination in 2004, Al Sharpton told black supporters, "We must no longer be the political mistress of the Democratic Party." Jonetta Rose Barras, an African American author, wrote in a commentary in the *Washington Post* in early 2004, "Some African Americans have accused the Democratic Party of practicing 'plantation politics' " and predicted that "the Democratic Party could lose its good thing." Yet although the political ground may be fertile for

Republicans to make inroads into the Democrat's near lock on black voters, until the vast majority of Republican leaders learn how to connect in a genuine way with black America, the GOP will have difficulty doing so. The party must work harder at doing this, in both deed and word.

Although African American voters constitute just 12 percent of the electorate, we must realize that the place race relations occupy in American life looms far larger than that. Given our history as a nation—and the moral imperative we have to make real the egalitarian democratic ideals of the country for every American—we cannot afford to write off black voters. Doing so is politically unwise and morally unjust. Solving the myriad and complex issues we face as a country demands the engagement of every single person, and that means blacks, whites, Hispanics, Asians, and others. The failure to attract any significant level of support from African American voters is also a major barrier to Republican efforts to become a true majority party, a party that represents the full cross section of Americans. Bob Dole was right when he said in 1996, "The Republican Party will never be whole until it earns the broad support of African-Americans and others by speaking to their hopes."

If the GOP is to deserve the support of African American and other minority voters—and help heal the harsh divisions of the country's current extreme partisanship—we must start talking and acting as if we seek and value that support. A good place to start would be to strongly and consistently repudiate offensive tactics and language used by any Republican candidate, officeholder, or organization at any time. As Abigail Thernstrom, a Republican

appointee to the United States Civil Rights Commission observed, "There have been a lot of self-inflicted wounds by the
Republican Party when it comes to race."

Let me cite just one example. Beginning in early 2003, groups
of College Republicans on numerous campuses around the country thought it would be a good idea to illustrate their opposition
to affirmative action in college admissions by holding a bake sale
at which white students would be charged a dollar for a cookie
while blacks and other minority students would be charged less.
This was supposed to illustrate the injustice of preferential treatment, but all it really did was make these Republicans look callous and small-minded. They offended their fellow students by
trivializing an important issue, and they reaffirmed the impression
that Republicans just don't understand these issues or how to discuss them. Affirmative action policies are certainly legitimate
subjects for debate, and reasonable people can disagree. But this
wasn't a debate; it was a cheap, offensive stunt that may have
made for good headlines, but did nothing to advance dialogue.
The failure by Republican leaders to denounce such sophomoric
and insensitive acts just reaffirms the negative view most African
Americans have of the GOP. It helps explain why, in a 2002
Gallup Poll that asked black Americans which party best reflected
"your values," 74 percent picked the Democratic Party, but just 6
percent picked the GOP.

It must be said that Republicans hardly have a monopoly on
offensive behavior. Racial insensitivity can be found on both sides
of the political aisle. In 2001, Senator Robert Byrd, a Democrat
from West Virginia and former member of the Ku Klux Klan, used
the term "white nigger" twice when being interviewed on a na-

tional news show. Democratic senator Fritz Hollings of South Carolina, who as the governor of that state in the early 1960s opposed the rights of African Americans to eat at whites-only lunch counters, has referred to Hispanics as "wetbacks," African diplomats as "potentates down from Africa [used to] eating each other," and a Jewish colleague as "the Senator from B'nai B'rith." Neither one of them paid any political price for his incredibly offensive remarks. In April 2004, in a widely ignored gaffe reminiscent of Trent Lott, Connecticut's senior senator, Democrat Christopher Dodd, paid tribute to the former KKK member Senator Robert Byrd by saying that he "would have been a great Senator at any moment" in America's history. I guess Dodd forgot that in one particular moment in history, Byrd was there on the Senate floor leading the filibuster against the Civil Rights Act of 1964—hardly a profile in courage; definitely not a moment of greatness.

There's no doubt that Democrats are given much more leeway when it comes to the politics of race. Trent Lott had to resign his post as majority leader because of a remark about Strom Thurmond. Yet despite his dismal record on civil rights, Robert Byrd was elected by Democrats as their majority leader, with hardly an eyebrow raised in protest. I do not believe for one minute that African American voters are any less offended by racially insensitive remarks when a Democrat makes them. I do believe, however, that the checkered pasts and callous remarks of Democrats are more likely to be overlooked or dismissed as an aberration because the Democratic Party, as a whole, is seen as more sympathetic to the concerns of African Americans.

Such reactions are frustrating to those of us in the Republican Party who have made a concerted effort to reach out to minorities, not only while running for office, but also in our governing. During the entire course of my political career, I have been quite intentional in such outreach, and I've been impressed by many of the party's recent efforts. Yet the fact is that those efforts tend to be seen as mere window dressing.

When the organizers of the Republican National Convention in the 2000 campaign made certain that African Americans and other minorities were featured prominently, the party was roundly criticized by Democrats—and many in the media—for tokenism. Yet in his first term, President George W. Bush appointed what is arguably the most diverse administration in history. His first cabinet included four women, two Asian Americans, two African Americans, and a Hispanic. When he appointed Colin Powell as secretary of state and Condoleezza Rice as national security adviser—making them the highest-ranking African Americans ever to serve in the executive branch—they were derided by some in the African American community as "sellouts" to their race.

This reaction is understandably frustrating to those in the Republican Party who are trying to do the right thing. It has limited the ability of the party to openly and creatively debate the concerns of African Americans and other minorities, just as it has also frustrated policy advances in some very important areas of concern to these groups. There's no doubt African Americans have allowed their votes to be taken for granted by the Democrats, thus weakening the leverage their community might have exercised on both parties over the years. President Bush made this point with passion and eloquence in his speech at the 2004 National Urban League Conference. "I know the Republican Party has got a lot of work to do. I understand that . . . I believe you've got to earn the vote and seek it. . . . And as I do, I'm going to ask African American voters to consider some questions. Does the Democrat Party take African American voters for granted? It's a fair question. I know plenty of politicians assume they have your vote. But do they earn it and do they deserve it? Is it a good thing for the African American community to be represented mainly by one political party? . . . How is it possible to gain political leverage if the party is never forced to compete? Have the traditional solutions of the Democrat Party truly served the African American community?"

I believe the Republican Party can make substantial progress in earning the respect and eventually the votes of African Americans. It can happen and the results can be worth it, as my experience has shown me time and again. Although Bill Clinton personally was wildly popular with black voters, they are much less enamored of John Kerry. In fact, several prominent African American Democratic leaders, including Donna Brazile, Al Gore's campaign manager in 2000, were openly critical of Kerry's failure to include blacks and other minorities in his inner circle, leading to his adding Jesse Jackson to his campaign in the last weeks before the election. Nevertheless, attracting the black vote will require more than rhetorical outreach by the Republicans.

I believe an important factor in the party's failure to make substantial progress in recent years in attracting minority votes is that Republicans at the national level still haven't learned to "think racially." I first heard that term from Buster Soaries, the former member of my gubernatorial cabinet whom I brought to the EPA to clear the backlog in discrimination cases. To make his point, Buster told me a story about the selection of bands for the parade that was to follow my inauguration as governor in 1993. At my request, the parade organizers were to make sure that each of New Jersey's twenty-one counties was represented in the parade by a high school marching band. So they set to work selecting the bands.

Without even thinking about it, every band they selected came from predominantly white high schools—even in those counties that have a majority black population, such as Essex County, where Newark is located. This happened because the people in charge of selecting the bands went to people they knew. It's a natural response—you have a job to do, you go to those you know can help you get it done. But in doing so, they didn't think racially, and in a state as diverse as New Jersey, that was inexcusable. They didn't consider how black parents in Newark, whose children were in their high school's marching band in the state's largest city, would feel when the governor's inaugural parade committee overlooked their children. Fortunately, because of the weather, the parade was canceled, but the committee's failure to ensure that the marching bands represented the state's diversity suggests just how much work we all have to do to work through the difficulties of racial division. I had appointed an inaugural event committee with little diversity.

A recent national example of the failure to think racially was George W. Bush's visit in 2004 to Atlanta to lay a wreath at the grave site of Dr. Martin Luther King, Jr., on Dr. King's birthday. When the visit was announced, it was immediately and vociferously denounced by many African Americans in Atlanta and elsewhere as disrespectful to Dr. King's memory. Why? Was it, at least in part, because the administration had given the impression that the visit was purely opportunistic and of a fairly low priority? After all, the visit was announced just days in advance—and after the president's reelection campaign had already announced he would be attending a fund-raiser in the Atlanta area. President Bush spent just fifteen minutes at the grave site, made no remarks, and left from there to attend the fund-raiser.

Contrast that to his father's visit, which also occurred at the start of an election year. Although some African American leaders had expressed concern about the elder Bush's policies and cynicism about the timing—and expressed those concerns forcefully to him at the event—he was respectfully received by Dr. King's family and the assembled crowd. The difference? The first President Bush's only stop in Atlanta that day was for the King remembrance. The event included remarks by members of Dr. King's family as well as by the president. Former President Carter was also in attendance, lending a bipartisan flavor to the event. It was also not the first time the elder Bush had commemorated Dr. King's birthday.

The clearest sense of how different the atmosphere was at the two events can be gleaned by comparing the headlines of the *Chicago Tribune*'s coverage of both events. In 1992 they wrote, BUSH, FOES UNITE TO HONOR KING; in 2004: CROWD JEERS BUSH AT M. L. KING'S TOMB. The *Trib*, by the way, endorsed both Bushes.

George W. Bush is not a racist. If he were, he would not have received more than one in four of African American votes when he ran for reelection as Texas governor (up from just 15 percent in his first campaign). I'm sure the Atlanta protesters had their own political motivations for criticizing him so harshly. But I understand the anger many African Americans felt about the way his visit was planned and carried out. As Julian Bond, head of the NAACP said, "I think it's a matter of timing. . . . We would have been pleased if the president had come two years ago or three years ago."

The White House later showed, however, that it could think racially. Four months after Dr. King's birthday, President Bush marked the fiftieth anniversary of the landmark *Brown v. Board of Education* ruling. He traveled to Topeka, Kansas, to dedicate the new *Brown v. Board of Education* National Historic Site, delivering an eloquent speech recognizing that although much progress has been made in eliminating racial discrimination in the United States, "the habits of racism in America have not all been broken." The five thousand people in attendance, including the Reverend Jesse Jackson, the chairman of the Congressional Black Caucus, and Cheryl Brown Henderson, the daughter of the lead plaintiff in the original lawsuit, warmly greeted the president. There was not a protester in sight. We've made far too little progress of this kind.

Many Republicans have concluded that the only issues African Americans and other minority groups care about are affirmative action, welfare, and affordable housing, which simply isn't true. I remember a dinner I hosted at the governor's residence for a group of about a dozen successful black entrepreneurs and business leaders. Throughout the evening, not a single person mentioned any of the so-called racial issues. What they wanted to discuss were economic issues—tax policy, trade opportunities, and access to capital.

The Republican philosophy on these issues should be one of our greatest strengths in winning back black voters and in attracting increasing support among other minority groups. As minority voters continue in greater numbers to climb the economic ladder, the Republican Party has a golden opportunity to speak with them about how our policies to stimulate economic growth will benefit all those who want to succeed. Robert Johnson, a Democrat and the founder and CEO of Black Entertainment Television, for example, has put together a coalition of black business leaders who favor repealing the inheritance tax, a position strongly supported by Republicans. Johnson believes that inheritance taxes make it more difficult for successful entrepreneurs to pass on their legacy of success to the next generation; so do Republicans. This is just one part of the larger Republican agenda to make it easier for America's families to create a better future for their children, but I think it also shows that we can find common ground in some unexpected places.

The Republican Party's initiative to provide grants to religious organizations should also engender strong support among African Americans. Certainly, the faith-based program we started in New Jersey in 1998 received strong support from that community. For generations, black churches have played a central role in the life of the African American community, including delivering social services to the needy. With federal funding for faith-based programs setting new records every year (more than $1.1 billion in fiscal year 2003), this is a perfect issue with which to reach out to African American voters, who tend to be more active in their churches and have more confidence in the ability of their religious institutions to make a difference in people's lives than any other group of Americans. Yet although funding faith-based programs enjoys strong support among black voters—one poll showed that more than 80 percent of African Americans supported such programs—Republicans have had trouble translating that support into a more constructive relationship with the African American community that could help break the lock Democrats have on African American votes.

In the case of education, it's the same story. Republicans have been in the lead in challenging what President Bush called the "soft bigotry of low expectations," promoting accountability through results, and providing opportunity for change. The No Child Left Behind Act, which the president signed in 2001, sets high expectations for all children and holds schools accountable when those expectations are not met. Republicans have been in the forefront of efforts to provide parents with educational choices for their children through such programs as vouchers and charter schools.

Early in my first term as governor, a black woman in Newark asked me, "Why shouldn't I have the same choice to send my children to a good school that you have?" It's a good question, and the Republican Party has some good answers. In New Jersey, as in many other states, Republicans have enacted laws that give parents that choice. Such programs attract significant support from African American voters. One recent poll showed that a majority of black voters (and two thirds of those with school-age children) support vouchers that would allow for school choice. Yet the Democrats have been strong and consistent opponents of vouchers; one might conclude that their loyalty to teachers unions, which are also firmly in the Democratic camp, exceeds their loyalty to their African American supporters. It took Congress more than eight years to fund a proposed school voucher program for students in Washington, D.C. Finally, in 2004, with the strong support of Washington's mayor and school board president—both black Democrats—Republicans succeeded in providing D.C. parents with thirteen million dollars in school vouchers for their children.

Success in earning the support of African American voters will take more than the efforts of a scattered few. The party must come together, at every level, and support a strategy that does more than pay lip service to the idea of attracting minority support. We must fully integrate minority voters into the fabric of the party and genuinely address their concerns; otherwise the deep skepticism about any attempts we make will surely persist, and it will continue to sour racial relations in the country. We must do the kind of job the Bush administration did so successfully with the Hispanic community through constant outreach and a focus on hiring Hispanics throughout the government.

During my own political career, I've seen that skepticism up close, as well as the lingering realities of racism that contribute to it. Explosive racial issues have, more than once, put my career in jeopardy, and those experiences have made me acutely aware of just how deeply and profoundly the racial divide continues to affect our politics. The success I've had in grappling with these issues has also convinced me of just how possible it is to make substantial progress.

The first time I was confronted with the intense volatility of racial politics was within days of my election as governor of New Jersey in 1993. Exactly a week after I was elected—becoming the first woman elected governor of my state and the first person to defeat an incumbent governor (Jim Florio) in a general election—

Ed Rollins, a highly paid and supposedly savvy political consultant who had worked on my campaign, met over breakfast with a group of reporters in Washington to discuss the election and my come-from-behind victory, for which he was eager to claim credit. Rollins bragged that my campaign had paid black ministers and mayors in New Jersey to suppress the vote in the African American community. He boasted that black ministers had been approached with offers to contribute money to their favorite charities if they would neglect to urge their congregants to vote on Election Day. He also said the campaign had offered to pay black mayors to "spend Election Day sitting at home watching television" instead of working to get out the vote. According to him, the campaign had funneled a total of half a million dollars to black clergy members and elected officials in these efforts,

It wasn't until later that day that I heard about what Rollins had said, and I was stunned. During the campaign, no one had ever suggested such an effort, and if someone had, I would have killed it (and probably her or him) immediately. But I also knew that in statewide campaigns, candidates do not always know everything that goes on, so I immediately got on the phone.

I called everyone who might know if such an effort—at any level by anyone affiliated with our campaign or the state party— had taken place. I called my brother Dan, who had played a big role in the campaign and had his finger on the pulse of everything that was going on. I then called our campaign treasurer, who would have to have known if that kind of money had gone out the door. Even in a multimillion-dollar campaign, it wouldn't be easy to hide half a million dollars. I also called our campaign's legal counsel, who made sure everything we did fully complied with

New Jersey's tough and complicated election laws. None of the dozen people I spoke with—including several African American friends and supporters who had served as senior advisers to my campaign from the beginning—had heard of any such thing.

I was far too angry to call Rollins directly (such a conversation would not have been constructive and would not have helped me get to the truth), so I had my most senior campaign officials talk to Rollins to find out exactly what he had said, and why. They reported back to me that Rollins said we shouldn't worry about what he had said—that it was no big deal and would quickly blow over. I didn't believe that for a minute, and as the number of calls from reporters grew throughout the day, it was clear I was right to be concerned.

The next day, papers from coast to coast and virtually every major television network reported Rollins's tale. The story was a political bombshell that not only threatened my election, but also threatened my ability to govern. If Rollins's story turned out to be true—even though I felt confident it wasn't—I would not have deserved to win the election. I also knew that even if the charges were found to be groundless, as they eventually were, the way in which I met this challenge would define everything I did for the rest of my career.

After assuring myself that the claims Rollins had made were not true, I called him. "What were you thinking?" I asked. He replied that he didn't know, and he asked me what he should do. I told him flat out, "You must say you lied—because you did." Within hours, Rollins issued a statement completely denying his claims, but by then it was too late; a political firestorm had been unleashed.

As the crisis exploded, I knew I had to act immediately and forcefully, not just to defend the integrity of my campaign, but also to defend the integrity of New Jersey's African American clergy and elected officials. After all, they'd been accused of selling out their congregations and constituents. It would have been impossible for me to work in the future with any members of New Jersey's minority community if I had not defended their integrity, as well as my own, and if I was to have any hope of successfully serving as governor, any doubts about the legitimacy of my election had to be put to rest completely and unquestionably.

When you find yourself in the midst of a firestorm like this, your instincts kick in. There isn't time to do a lot of planning or seek a wide variety of advice. Things are happening too quickly. You have to rely on what you think is right—and hope for the best. So the first thing I did was to go before the press and express my own outrage at what Rollins said had gone on. I didn't try to defend him or his behavior in any way, and I made sure everyone connected with my campaign took the same approach. There were to be no carefully worded statements designed to give us wiggle room in case it turned out someone on my campaign had done what Rollins had alleged.

The Democrats smelled blood in the water, and they were determined to do whatever they could to try to capitalize on Rollins's incredible stupidity. I was surprised, however, that they didn't seem to understand that in their rush to condemn me, they were also attacking the integrity of New Jersey's black clergy.

The turning point came the next day, just two days after the story broke. Through the press, my office learned that the Reverend Jesse Jackson and the Reverend Al Sharpton were coming to Trenton, New Jersey's capital, to attend a rally at which they would discuss a possible lawsuit for slander against Rollins, my campaign, and the New Jersey Republican State Committee. When I heard that these two leaders would be in Trenton, set to lead a march on my transition office, I immediately placed a call to Jackson and invited both him and Sharpton to meet with me before the rally.

We met in a small conference room in the back of the modest suite of offices the state provides a governor-elect. The meeting was small: Jackson; Sharpton; just two of my senior campaign advisers, Herb Tate and Lonna Hooks, who are both African American; and me. The conversation, as they say in diplomatic circles, was frank. Somewhat to my surprise, Sharpton—who is a New Jersey resident and had earlier in the day appeared at a press conference in Newark with other black clergy members denouncing me in no uncertain terms—seemed to be the most interested in finding a way to go forward together. Both were understandably outraged, but Sharpton seemed to acutely appreciate that if someone had been giving bribes, someone else had to be taking them. If Rollins's charge was true, it was troublesome not just for my campaign, but also for their clergy colleagues as well.

So here I was, not even sworn in as governor, meeting face to face with the two most influential black political activists in the country in what was most definitely not a get-acquainted session. I knew that simple denials would not be enough, so I took a gamble. I assured Jackson and Sharpton that if the various investigations looking into the claims supported Rollins's allegation, I would agree to a new election for governor and that I was prepared to leave that meeting and say that to the huge crush of press gathering in a room down the hall. Jesse Jackson expressed some reluctance, but Al Sharpton was willing to give me a chance. In exchange for my pledge to vacate the election if Rollins's charges were proven true, they agreed to call off their planned demonstration. We went out to meet the press.

The press conference itself remains a blur to me. It was one of those moments when time seems to stand still but also race by at warp speed. The reporters seemed to have a hard time accepting that the demonstration was being postponed, and they were surprised that Jackson and Sharpton were willing to wait for the results of the investigations before declaring the election invalid. That's how deep the cynicism among the press corps was. This wasn't how it was supposed to turn out; they were going to have to rewrite their stories.

Now the wait began. There were at least half a dozen investigations under way and a Justice Department hotline for anyone who had anything to add to the discussion. Perhaps what I understand least from those days (beyond a reason why Rollins would ever have said such a thing) was why there never was, to my knowledge (and I would have heard about it), even one recorded call to the hotline. Usually, when law enforcement sets up a tip line, you can count on any number of crank calls and malicious mischief makers, but this line stayed silent. For that I am eternally grateful. It would have taken just one person trying to make trouble to tip the balance against me.

If I learned anything from those days and weeks, it was that reaching out to even the most partisan people is sometimes worth the effort. I am convinced that a lesson I learned during my days running the Listening Program—that even when meeting with people who were fully prepared to oppose you, you could at least moderate their readiness to attack you if you would truly hear them out—prepared me for that meeting with Jackson and Sharpton.

The fact that during the campaign I had made an effort to reach out for the support of African Americans also helped me survive this crisis. I had campaigned in black neighborhoods, even though some of my advisers had told me it was a waste of time and could even be counterproductive because it might encourage turnout against me. As it turned out I carried 25 percent of the black vote in that first election. So when on the first Sunday after the story broke I attended services at two black churches, I was not derided as a Johnny-come-lately showing up only when I needed political cover. It was heartening to read in news accounts that one church congregant had said, "She is very welcome here," and another told a reporter, "It's a good sign that she came here. It shows that she is the candidate for everybody." A week after the firestorm started, it had largely died down, but I had learned an invaluable lesson and was determined to continue—and even expand—the outreach efforts I had made during the campaign.

For outreach to minority communities to be effective, it must be sincere and sustained. I made it clear, even before I took office as governor, that promoting respect for all New Jerseyans would be a signature effort of my administration. The Saturday night before my inauguration, we held a huge Ethnic Pride and Heritage Festival in Atlantic City. In my first year as governor, we established the Many Faces-One Family program to promote diversity and respect for the scores of growing ethnic groups that call New Jersey home. I attended a host of ethnic festivals and celebrations, and in the dozens of visits I made to classrooms, I incorporated a message about tolerance and respect. I also named many women and minorities to important posts, including some of the highest positions in state government—roles in which women and minorities had never before served.

Many skeptics scoff at efforts such as these as meaningless symbolism. Plenty of people took pot shots at me on election night in 1993, when I wore a kente cloth that an African American supporter had given me on the campaign trail. I have seen throughout my career, however, that symbolic acts by political leaders can carry great meaning. In the fall of 1995, I attended an event with Indian Americans. When I arrived, I was greeted with a traditional welcoming ceremony called *aarathi*, which included placing a *bindi*, a brightly colored dot, on my forehead. I didn't think much of it, besides feeling just a bit awkward, but the five hundred people in attendance were deeply moved. They remembered that just a few years before, in a nearby town, Indian women wearing bindi were being beaten up or verbally harassed in something the perpetrators were calling dot busting. To see their governor putting on a bindi assured them that I supported their right to live peacefully and safely. This symbolic act was reported in an Indian newspaper under the headline GOV. WHITMAN PUTS AN END TO "DOT BUSTER" ERA.

Symbolism is not sufficient unless you also confront racism in the strongest terms and do something serious about it. I had my chance, and it involved one of the most sacrosanct of institutions, the New Jersey State Police.

For literally decades in New Jersey, minorities had been complaining that the state police were targeting them because of their race. Going back for at least three previous governors—of both parties—charges had been made that New Jersey state troopers were unfairly stopping minority motorists on the state's major roads, and subjecting them to unwarranted searches. In order to address discriminatory conduct by troopers on New Jersey's highways, the state attorney general and the head of the New Jersey State Police had taken steps three years before I took office to change the standard operating procedures state troopers used in making roadside stops. At the time, my Democratic predecessor's acting attorney general thought those changes had addressed the problem effectively.

As odious as it is, racial profiling is not easy to define. Criminal profiling has long been an accepted practice of law enforcement and an essential part of police work—but only when used effectively. After the terrorist attacks of September 11, when it became clear that every one of the hijackers was a young Arab male, it was tempting to think we could prevent further attacks by concentrating our law enforcement efforts on those who appeared to be young Arab males. The problem with that is twofold. First, you end up using an enormous amount of resources going after a lot of innocent people. Second, the terrorists could (and do) easily change tactics, using people with a different ethnic or gender profile to carry out their next attack. So unless you know, for certain, what the general appearance of future attackers will be, profiling is of only limited use.

As governor, I understood that law enforcement is a tough job and that the men and women who put on the uniform risk their lives every day to keep our roads and communities safe. They are often confronted with split-second decisions that can mean the difference between life and death. If someone pulls a gun on a police officer, that officer doesn't have the luxury of time to figure out whether it's a real or toy gun, and whether it's loaded or unloaded. The officer has to react. That's why elected officials are reluctant—and they should be—to micromanage the ways in which the police do their jobs.

I had visited the bedsides of too many state troopers injured or shot in the line of duty, comforted too many young trooper widows, and attended too many memorial services to presume that politicians could do the jobs of police officers better than they could. In addition, I had always instinctively felt—and had no reason to believe otherwise—that if I hadn't done anything wrong, I had nothing to fear from the police. Clearly, however, African Americans and other minorities often don't have that comfort. They have learned, through bitter experience, that being a law-abiding citizen isn't always enough to protect them from harassment by law enforcement.

Just such harassment was alleged in an incident that occurred late on the evening of April 23, 1998, when four young men—three black and one Hispanic—were traveling in a 1997 Dodge Caravan on the New Jersey Turnpike to a college basketball tryout in North Carolina. They were pulled over by a pair of state troopers on routine patrol, ostensibly for exceeding the speed limit by almost twenty miles per hour. After the driver had pulled off onto the shoulder of the road, the troopers exited their patrol car and began to walk toward the van. They claimed that as they approached, the van suddenly backed up toward them at a high rate of speed, knocking one of them to the ground. The troopers responded by firing their weapons, discharging eleven rounds into the van and wounding three of the four occupants, one seriously.

As the event was investigated, the troopers' response was revealed to have been grossly disproportionate to the threat they thought they had faced. Witnesses came forward to state that the van was just rolling (not speeding) backward; others appeared to question the troopers' stated reason for making the stop in the first place, claiming that the van was not traveling much, if at all, above the speed limit. This tragedy, which became known simply as the Turnpike Shooting, quickly became national news. As time went on, and I learned more about the events of that night and the records of the troopers involved, I became convinced that the many assurances offered by the state police to my predecessors and to me were not entirely reliable. There seemed to be, at some barracks and among some groups of troopers, an effort to target African American and Hispanic drivers, mainly because of their ethnicity.

The investigation was launched within days of the shooting. Although I knew how important it was that justice be allowed to pursue its course along normal channels, I also knew I was confronting an issue much larger than the fate of these two troopers. If racial discrimination was a pattern, it drove to the very heart of the integrity of the state police as an organization. What I had to determine was whether state troopers were profiling motorists because of their race and whether that behavior was known to and thus tolerated or even encouraged by state police leadership.

Many in the African American community, including the Black Ministers Council, were quick to issue demands for an immediate, far-reaching probe. I understood their desire to move as soon as possible, but I did not want to compromise whatever case might be developed in the Turnpike Shooting case by short-circuiting the judicial process. A grand jury had been impaneled to investigate the shootings, and it had to be given time to do its work.

I did make certain, however, that the head of the state police knew how strongly I opposed the practice of racial profiling and how swiftly I would act to eradicate it if it was shown to exist. In the months following the shooting, the superintendent of the state police, Colonel Carl Williams (himself a career trooper), said all the right things, both to me and to the public. Yet I had nagging doubts about how deep his commitment went and whether he was truly communicating the need for change down the ranks. Unfortunately, my concerns were confirmed at a summit I convened in December 1998 to explore police-community relations throughout the State of New Jersey.

This was the first time that the police and the minority community had come together to share their concerns, and it began a useful dialogue that should have happened much earlier. I distinctly remember that when the Reverend Reginald Jackson, the executive director of the Black Ministers Council, asked Colonel Williams point-blank to acknowledge that there had been a problem, Colonel Williams just sat there not responding, as uncomfortable as I've ever seen anyone in my life. The summit, and the Colonel's obvious discomfort, reaffirmed in my mind the need to move forward and get to the truth.

Within months of the shooting, we had installed video cameras in more than two hundred patrol cars that would turn on automatically whenever a trooper turned on his or her emergency lights, recording everything that happened during a stop. Despite initial resistance from some troopers, time and again the cameras were to prove their effectiveness. They protected troopers from false accusations and protected motorists by deterring stops that would not have been appropriate. We put in place a plan to install cameras, not just in state police cars, but in local patrol cars as well. Unfortunately, my Democratic successor scuttled the plan (without any protest from the Black Ministers Council).

In addition, in response to a media request, the state police undertook a review of their arrest records on the turnpike for a two-month period in 1997 to compile numbers about the race or ethnicity of those who had been arrested. The results of the review, when they were released in February 1999, were so dramatic that they surprised me and shook the state police to its core. During the period reviewed, 75 percent of those arrested on the turnpike were minorities. This number was ludicrously high. I had spent enough hours traveling the turnpike to know that minority drivers didn't constitute anywhere near three quarters of the drivers; in fact, one subsequent study showed that a little more than 35 percent of those traveling on the turnpike are minorities.

Almost immediately, my administration launched a comprehensive investigation into the state police to determine whether recruitment, training, promotions, organizational structure, and other issues could be creating or contributing to a culture that either promoted or tolerated racial discrimination. This included looking into not just whether racial profiling was being practiced (which it certainly appeared to be), but also how widespread it was and whether the force's leadership was supporting it in any way.

I wanted the investigation to be completed and a report on my desk within four months.

Shortly after that, I met with black ministers to hear their concerns and tell them about the details of the investigation. I assured them that once the report was completed, I would follow it wherever it led—and if that meant major changes in the state police, that's what would happen. The Reverend Reginald Jackson told one reporter he would be "absolutely amazed" if the report did not uncover evidence of racial profiling. And by then, I'd have been amazed myself.

Then the superintendent of the state police, Colonel Williams, gave an interview to a major statewide paper that revealed that the problem started right at the top of the force. Under the headline TROOPER BOSS: RACE PLAYS ROLE IN DRUG CRIMES, Colonel Williams betrayed a stunning lack of awareness about what racial profiling was and just how wrong it was. In what might have been the understatement of the year, the reporter wrote, "In remarks that are likely to fuel further controversy over the State Police, Superintendent Carl Williams in an interview late last week said he detests the targeting of minorities on the New Jersey Turnpike, but that it would be naive to think race is not an issue in drug trafficking." I was shocked as I read on and found Williams making the most sweeping generalizations linking minorities to broad categories of criminal activities—statements that proved to me beyond any doubt that although his intentions might have been right, he did not have the faintest idea what the problem really was, let alone how to address it. It was clear that Williams had to go, a fact that he apparently understood as well. After a call from the attorney general, Williams submitted his resignation.

I took no pleasure in Colonel Williams's resignation. I had appointed him superintendent five years earlier, and he had compiled an honorable record during more than thirty years in the state police. He was hardly the only law enforcement officer in the nation to fail to understand how insidious racial profiling could be. Even the federal Drug Enforcement Administration—an arm of the Justice Department—had issued guidelines for identifying potential drug suspects that endorsed the use of broadly drawn racial and ethnic characteristics as a legitimate law enforcement technique. Yet I was committed to ensuring that New Jersey's law enforcement system was both effective and free of bias, and his comments, and the lack of understanding they conveyed, were completely inconsistent with our efforts to meet that commitment.

The reaction to Williams's resignation was swift. Minority leaders, as I expected, expressed satisfaction that he had resigned, but they kept a wait-and-see attitude about whether it would lead to reform. The rank-and-file troopers, on the other hand, were quick to lionize Williams as the victim of political correctness and attack me for selling them out. Much of the goodwill I had earned by enacting such tough anticrime laws as No Early Parole, Three Strikes and You're In, and the Police Officers' Bill of Rights, and by adding new troopers to the force (after my predecessor had frozen hiring), disappeared almost overnight. To protest, troopers on highway patrol staged a work slowdown in March, writing only a third as many tickets as they had the previous March. In addition, I came under heavy attack from right-wingers who charged me with putting political correctness ahead of crime fighting.

Eventually, we also learned that not only were some troopers systematically practicing racial profiling, but they were also making deliberate efforts to cover it up. As part of the probe, we sent investigators to meet with a large sample of motorists who had been pulled over on certain sections of the turnpike where a statistical analysis had suggested that racial profiling might be taking place. On numerous occasions, the investigators met with someone whose race was listed as white on the state police paperwork, only to find that the person was in fact an African American or another minority.

The report ultimately concluded that although the vast majority of state troopers did not practice racial profiling, the behavior was real and there was a subculture that tolerated it. On the basis of the report, we put together a plan of action that took numerous steps to root out the practice, and we entered into a consent decree with the U.S. Department of Justice in a process that allowed them to monitor our progress—the first such agreement in the country.

With that report, New Jersey became the first state in the nation to admit that racial profiling was "real, not imagined" and to systematically investigate charges of racial profiling. Being the first to tackle this thorny issue, however, didn't pay any immediate political dividends. Democrats were quick to attack me for not undertaking the investigation earlier. Republican officeholders were muted in their response, neither praising us for unearthing the truth, nor criticizing us for not doing something sooner. I believe that most of them, prizing their credentials as strong anticrime legislators, didn't want to incite political reprisals from law enforcement organizations; others thought we were persecuting the state police to win political points among minority voters. The most measured response came from New Jersey's prominent African American leaders, the Black Ministers Council. Although African American Democrats in the legislature were quick to attack me as insincere and too late, and sought to use the profiling to their advantage, the council's executive director, Rev. Reginald Jackson, told the press, "[W]e celebrate that the problem of profiling has been acknowledged."

I thought a Miami-based truck driver who had been traveling the turnpike for years best put the challenge before us. "I want them to see a black man driving the turnpike with Florida plates and think: 'There's a hardworking guy.'" That day may finally have come. In early 2004, the superintendent of the state police (who was appointed by my successor, a Democrat) reported that since the steps my administration had initiated were put in place, not a single case of racial profiling had been reported. Rev. Jackson of the New Jersey Black Ministers Council was quoted as saying about accusations of racial profiling. "It's something we don't even hear anymore." Real progress can be made with real effort.

Unfortunately, this success story is all too unusual. New Jersey remains the only state to have undertaken a comprehensive review of the incidence of racial profiling. This is unfortunate but not surprising. Because many politicians find racial politics so difficult to navigate, few in either party are eager to take on the tough problems. They know all too well just how quickly rhetoric becomes inflamed and passions are ignited. One false move can be disastrous, as one especially unfortunate move of mine nearly was.

When I first became governor, the most pressing urban problem we faced was the plight of the city of Camden. A once-proud and prosperous manufacturing city (anyone who's ever enjoyed a can of Campbell's tomato soup has enjoyed a Camden product), Camden's decades-long economic and social decline was so complete that it had become known as the Murder Capital of New Jersey, and it was one of the five poorest cities in the nation. I asked the attorney general and the state police to determine how best we could help, and they proposed the creation of a special state police task force to help break the back of the drug trade that was behind so much of the crime. So in the fall of 1995 we sent the state police into Camden.

As was my habit ever since I had first entered elected office more than a decade before, I planned to see for myself exactly what was going on out in the field. So I arranged to ride with the state police's special teams on their nighttime patrols on two separate nights to see what we were up against. It was an eye-opener. I had been to the city several times before, but never at night. It was an entirely different place after dark. Seeing abandoned and boarded-up houses by day is troubling enough. Driving those same streets and seeing just one house lit up in a block of darkness is positively chilling. The noise of everyday traffic is nothing compared to the sounds of lookouts warning the drug dealers that we were coming.

I didn't just watch from the van as the troopers did their work; I went with them into boarded-up houses and saw the booby traps that had been laid to injure the police and give the occupants a chance to escape. I walked with them into basements that had been fitted out as drug dens, with small holes bored through concrete walls to allow the transfer of drugs without letting anyone gain access to the space. Those two nights provided an education I never could have gotten in an office, and the direct experience made a difference. That learning experience, however, would come back to haunt me.

More than once during those two nights, the troopers had said to me, "Nobody back at the barracks is ever going to believe us when we tell them you were out here with us." So when, toward the end of the second night, they asked me if I would mind having my picture taken patting down a suspect, I foolishly agreed. I wasn't thinking racially; in fact, I wasn't thinking. As soon as I touched the young man, who was African American, I realized I'd made a mistake. I had no business "fake frisking" him. A photo was quickly snapped, the young man (who hadn't recognized me) was allowed to go on his way, and we climbed back into the van and drove away. Four years later, that picture made national news.

On Saturday, July 8, 2000, I sat down to read the morning papers and there was that photo, on page one. I had learned the day before that several news outlets had been given the photo and were planning to run it the next morning, and I knew it was going to be a problem, but until I saw it there, splashed across page one, I didn't fully appreciate just how big a problem it would be.

The timing of this release was no accident. My administration was in the midst of our effort to reform the state police, and the frisk photo appeared just weeks before the Republican National Convention was scheduled to open in Philadelphia, right across the Delaware River from where the picture had been taken. At that time there was talk that I might be under consideration as a possible vice-presidential candidate (I never took that talk seriously because I didn't think a pro-choice Republican had a chance of being nominated). Obviously, someone in the state police had leaked the photo to embarrass me at what was thought to be a particularly critical time. As one out-of-state African American activist put it, "A picture's worth a thousand words. It might be worth a vice presidential nomination."

This incident illustrates the value of building genuine relationships in the African American community. Although New Jersey Democrats were quick to label me a racist, New Jersey's most prominent black leaders did not. Rev. Jackson, head of the Black Ministers Council of New Jersey, demanded a full explanation from me, but he also told a reporter, "I would vehemently disagree with anybody who says that the Governor is a racist. I have no inclination to believe that at all." He went on to say, "I think it is very callous and very cynical of whoever in the State Police held them for four years, to bring [the photo] out at this time." Because I had developed thoughtful relationships and a record of progress on the race relations front—not just the occasional outreach to minority communities, but a track record of actively listening to minorities' concerns and working with them on a sincere basis—I had earned enough goodwill to see me through.

What was most important, though, was that by working with minority populations, my administration had achieved some important policy objectives that otherwise might not have gone forward. We were able to put in place a faith-based community initiative that helped direct much-needed resources into numerous minority neighborhoods, building on the job training, educational opportunities, and mentoring that their own communities were able to provide. We were able to enact a welfare reform proposal that not only shrank the welfare rolls, but also gave welfare recipients assistance in finding and keeping jobs—for many, for the first time in their adult lives. We were able to initiate reform in the state police, and we were able to increase funding for schools in New Jersey's most disadvantaged districts. We had done a lot of good work in urban minority communities such as Camden, Newark, and Elizabeth, from providing new stocks of affordable housing to spending hundreds of millions of dollars to improve schools and neighborhoods. In short, we were able to get beyond the shouting that too often animates conversations about race and really address the issues. And we were able to do it as Republicans.

The legacy of Lincoln is a proud one. While truly reasserting our claim to the title will be neither easy nor swift, Republicans must make the effort. The racial and ethnic makeup of our increasingly diverse country means that any party that wants to remain relevant—and that deserves the opportunity to lead—must embrace America's rich diversity and engage all its people, speaking to their hopes and dreams for the future of their families and of our country.

CHAPTER FIVE

This Land Is Our Land

"Too often, the Republican Party has been defeated by an unwill-ingness or an inability to speak to important issues of the day. Issues that matter to Americans. Issues like the environment. . . . If we are to be the national majority party we aspire, it is incumbent on us to speak to these issues and speak with a clear voice."

GOVERNOR TOM RIDGE, 1999

All my life I've spent as much time as possible enjoying the outdoors. Whether I'm hiking, kayaking, fishing, mountain biking, riding, or just taking in the beauty of nature, I find that nothing restores the body, mind, and spirit like being outdoors. One of the hardest parts about being out of office and working in my home office at my farm is staying focused on work—I'd much rather be outside with the dogs.

Both of my parents loved nature and open space. The farm on which I grew up had been given to them by my mother's parents as a wedding present. They called it Pontefract (which means "broken bridge") after the English town from which my father's family had come to America. It's a beautiful place nestled in the rolling hills of western New Jersey, about fifty miles outside New York City, but really a world away. They raised four children on it and tended the land with great care, eventually closing out their long and productive lives there.

After my parents died, my husband and I were fortunate enough to be able to purchase the farm from their estate and make it our own home. As I write this, I'm sitting in my office on the second floor of the barn, overlooking a pasture where my daughter's old pony, Melody, is grazing as I gaze across to the apple orchard my father planted decades ago.

My father loved trees, and I can remember him planting hundreds of them over the years. My mother used to tease him, reminding him that more than a century earlier some poor farmer had spent hours of backbreaking labor clearing that land of trees, and now here he was, planting them by the score. I can still picture him, at age eighty, tearing vines down out of "his trees" to prevent the vines from strangling their branches.

Pontefract was and is a working farm. Its main crop has always been hay, but my parents also grew grain and oats at various times over the years. I remember all too well the hot, sweaty, dusty job of bringing in the hay and stacking the bales in the hayloft. Today, when I see giant rolls of hay in fields, looking like some sort of rolled pastry on steroids, my mind slips back to how hard it was to bring in the hay, but how much fun we had as children playing in the hayloft.

My parents believed that there is a certain democracy about farm life, and that it didn't matter whether you were the farm owner, the farmhand, or even the farmer's daughter; when there was work be done, everyone had to pitch in and do it. Among the skills they taught me were the fine art of mucking out stalls, the proper way to groom a horse, and how to tell when a cow, horse, or pig is about to give birth.

Some of my fondest early memories are of chasing after wayward chickens, riding my pony, Stuffy, and fishing for catfish and sunnies (and the rare trout) in the stream that ran through our property. Now and again, my father, brothers, and I would stretch an old fishing net across the stream and drag it along the stream bed up to our property line in a futile effort to decrease the population of snapping turtles that were constantly getting the better of the ducks that lived along the banks. Before my parents put in a pool, we'd also swim in the stream, always taking along a handful of salt from the kitchen, which we'd use to remove the leeches that would inevitably attach themselves to our limbs.

My mother would often refer to our barn as Noah's Ark. They raised Jersey milking cows, Hereford beef cattle, and pigs—always pigs—the most efficient disposers of wet trash known to man. Our many well-fed sows regularly attracted the attention of our neighbor's boar Topper. Topper was enormous; I can recall, as a child, riding him around the barnyard. I will never forget the time I opened the door to the barn and found myself nose to nose with Topper, who was making an unplanned visit. Before he had a chance to charge, I was off like a shot.

My favorite time of year on the farm has always been August. The heat of July is starting to become a memory as the days slowly grow shorter and the nights become just a bit cooler. August is also the time of year when we can live for the entire month off the produce and meat we raise. John always says we could eat every night of the year in the most expensive New York restaurant for what its costs us to raise everything, but no meal I've ever had in the finest restaurant equals those August dinners at the farm.

At the center of family life on Pontefract Farm is the white clapboard farmhouse, the oldest part of which was built in 1769. Over the years it's been expanded and changed to meet the needs of the various families who've called it home, rambling off to one side and the other. It's not a grand house, but it's roomy and its many windows let in plenty of light. It's a house filled with many memories, and I'm always pleased when a visitor compliments it by calling it a warm and comfortable home. As a girl, my bedroom was on the second floor, overlooking the grape arbor and the small lawn that abuts it. On many a spring morning I would be awakened by the distinctive whirring and clicking of our hand-powered reel lawn mower, which Ma was pushing back and forth across the grass. On really hot summer nights we would decamp to the upstairs sleeping porch (the house has never been centrally air conditioned), where the rhythmic sounds of peepers, crickets, and cicadas would lull us to sleep, punctuated by the occasional insistent midnight call of a mockingbird.

Although our farm was not the main source of my parents' income, it defined the rhythm of their day-to-day life. My father was never happier than when he came home from a long day in New York City and could spend a few hours on the seat of his tractor mowing a field. I always felt that when he exchanged his suit and tie for his well-worn work clothes, he felt more fulfilled than at any other time, even more than when he was collaborating with captains of industry on big building projects or working behind the scenes on political causes.

As much as my parents loved our farm, they also enjoyed exploring the greater outdoors. Nearly every summer during my childhood, we'd travel out west for vacation, more often than not spending a week on a ranch in Idaho, Montana, or Wyoming. These were active vacations spent riding horses, shooting skeet, fishing some of America's greatest trout streams, sleeping in a bedroll out under the skies.

Perhaps my most memorable experience out west was on the Two-Slash-Spear Ranch in Pinedale, Wyoming, when I was fourteen. The rancher took on five or six girls that summer to do his haying, and I was one of them. As part of our experience, he took us on a two-week pack trip into the Wind River Mountains. It was a rigorous trip: at one point one of our pack horses lost his footing and disappeared over the edge of the trail; fortunately, we were able to recover him (although his load was gone forever). Every night we'd sleep under the stars, and each morning we'd catch our breakfast (usually trout) and cook it over an open fire. Because the trip took place in August, we were treated every clear night to the sight of what seemed like millions of shooting stars— the Perseid meteor showers. I can still picture the way the entire vault of the sky would be filled with stars. I thought back to those wonderful nights in Wyoming when I was at the EPA and we took steps to reduce the haze that has drastically limited the views in so many of our national parks in recent years. For example, 120 years ago, visitors to the Great Smoky Mountains could see for 100 miles on a clear day. Today, because of air pollution, that view has been slashed to just 20 miles on the clearest of days.

My father told me at an early age, "Always leave any place you go cleaner than you found it." That ethic, and my lifelong immersion in the rhythms and beauty of nature, has instilled me with the deep commitment to environmental protection that so many Americans share.

It seems only natural, then, that I should have found a home in the Republican Party. Beginning with the establishment of the national parks system by Theodore Roosevelt, Republicans have been in the forefront of environmental protection for the past one hundred years. In fact, the story of the modern approach to environmental protection is largely a story of Republican leadership and vision.

For much of the twentieth century, environmentalism was known by another name—conservation. As America began to spread west rapidly after the discovery of gold in California in 1848 and the completion of the transcontinental railroad two decades later, many Americans began to worry about the fate of our country's great natural treasures. Beginning with Teddy Roosevelt's presidency, the nation began to accept an environmental ethic that acknowledged an obligation to conserve America's magnificent landscape even as the country grew into the world's most powerful industrial economy. As the economy boomed, the threats to the environment became even more pressing, and it eventually became clear that conservation was not enough—the federal government would have to act.

The first major warning sign that environmental degradation was becoming a national threat occurred in October 1948, as toxic emissions from a zinc works in Donora, Pennsylvania, a mining town of fourteen thousand in the Monongahela Valley, became trapped by a thermal inversion—in effect a massive smog cloud—that had settled over the town. Within just six days, half the town's population fell ill or was hospitalized, and twenty people died. Today, this tragic event is seen as one of the early labor pains that eventually led to the birth in 1970, on the first Earth Day, of the modern environmental ethos.

Over the past thirty-five years, the vast majority of federal programs and policies that have improved the condition of our environment are the legacies and accomplishments of Republican presidents and their administrations. The National Environmental Policy Act (Nixon), the Clean Air Act (Nixon), the Endangered Species Act (Nixon), the Safe Drinking Water Act (Ford), the Toxic Substances Control Act (Ford), the Emergency Planning and Community Right to Know Act (Reagan), the Superfund Amendments and Reauthorization Act (Reagan), the Oil Pollution Act of 1990 (Bush 41), the Pollution Prevention Act (Bush 41), and the Brownfields Revitalization Act (Bush 43) are just some of the laws that have made a real difference in the quality of America's environment.

Yet in recent years, despite actually supporting a good deal of important environmental protection legislation, the Republican Party's reputation as a steward of the environment has dramatically deteriorated, and the party is now widely perceived by the American public as downright antienvironment. Throughout 2004, national polls showed that voters had significantly more confidence in the Democrats' commitment to protecting the environment than they did in the GOP. When asked which party they believed would do a better job protecting the environment, an NBC News-*Wall Street Journal* poll revealed that only 18 percent had more faith in Republicans, whereas 51 percent put more stock in the Democrats. One Gallup Poll reported that Americans favored Democrats over Republicans on environmental matters by 22 points—the largest margin of any of the issues considered. Another Gallup Poll showed that 59 percent of the American people believe the claims of scientists that the Bush administration is "ignoring or distorting scientific evidence about environmental problems," whereas not even one third believed the administration was telling the truth. When the *Newsweek* poll asked voters which presidential candidate could do a better job handling the environment, Kerry posted his largest margin over Bush on any of the issues listed—59 to 29. The only good news for Republicans in all this data is that the environment ranks relatively low on lists of voter concerns. Of course that doesn't mean the public isn't in fact strongly in support of environmental protection. It is, and the reputation the party has developed on this issue should trouble all Republicans.

One of the real tragedies in this is that hundreds of Republican leaders—at every level of government—have built strong environmental records that reflect the GOP's tradition of environmental stewardship. Republican governors ranging from veterans such as George Pataki in New York and Jeb Bush in Florida to those more recently elected, including Tim Pawlenty in Minnesota and Arnold Schwarzenegger in California, are compiling positive, progressive environmental records. Republicans in Congress, including representatives Jim Greenwood of Pennsylvania, Fred Upton of Michigan, Sherry Boehlert of New York, and senators Dick Lugar of Indiana and Gordon Smith of Oregon, along with many others, have taken strong, principled stands on behalf of environmental protection. Unfortunately, the contributions these Republicans, and many more like them, have made are overshadowed by the national reputation the party suffers from on environmental issues.

The harsh assessment of the party's record and stand on the environment is due in part to the ridiculously extreme rhetoric used by all sides in what passes for debate on environmental issues these days. Environmental groups in particular have attacked the Republican Party in ways that would be ruled out of order on any school yard in America. The once reasonable National Wildlife Federation wasted no time in demanding, less than three months after he took office, that President Bush "End [His] War on the Environment." The Natural Resources Defense Council claimed that, "This administration, in catering to industries that put America's health and natural heritage at risk, threaten to do more damage to our environmental protections than any other in U.S. history." The Sierra Club's bias is reflected in where they make their campaign contributions: They gave nearly five hundred thousand dollars to Democratic House and Senate candidates in 2002 and less than twenty thousand dollars to Republican candidates that same year. Is it any wonder Republicans find groups like these difficult to work with? Rhetoric like theirs is counterproductive—it gets in the way of constructive policy making.

On the other hand, the rhetoric thrown around by many prominent Republicans certainly hasn't helped either. When the Republican chairman of the Senate Environment and Public Works Committee calls EPA's career staff—a group of people I found to be dedicated, intelligent public servants—"a Gestapo bureaucracy"; or when the vice president remarked, shortly after being named to chair the President's Energy Task Force, "Conservation may be a sign of personal virtue, but it is not a sufficient basis for a sound, comprehensive energy policy"; or when the Senate Republican leader defends the wasteful use of oil as a "right"—it's no wonder so many people today feel they have reason to doubt the party's commitment to the environment.

Anytime you seek to redress an imbalance in policy, or change the status quo, people are going to object. What's unfortunate is the degree to which the highly charged atmosphere that surrounds environmental issues has made reasonable debate almost impossible. Nowhere has this been clearer than in the discussion over an administration proposal to open the Arctic National Wildlife Refuge (ANWR) to oil exploration.

Just as reasonable people can muster arguments against the proposal, so too can a reasonable argument be made that such exploration can be undertaken without destroying the sensitive ecology of the refuge. In February 2004, *Outside* magazine tried to contribute to the debate by publishing an article titled "Crude Reality," which tried to make the case for permitting exploration in ANWR. Among the conclusions the author reached was that "both sides are too entrenched to see the other side clearly." Little did he know. Letters to the editor poured in, many of them taking the magazine to task for even running the article. "Shame on you," one writer wrote. " 'Crude Reality' is the biggest piece of shit *Outside* has ever published," penned another. The response reached such a fevered pitch that the magazine's editor felt compelled to issue a statement that said, in part, "Given how polarized and even mutually uncomprehending the two sides of this debate have become, we realized that many readers will strongly disagree with both [the author's] recommendations in 'Crude Reality' and with *Outside*'s decision to publish the story. But it is our view that the final outcome of the dispute should not be achieved through poisonous invective, but through a healthy and open discussion of the facts on both sides." Unfortunately, that view is in the minority when it comes to environmental debate in America today.

The Republican Party has a strong argument to make that many environmental regulations have become counterproductive expenses on businesses and state and local governments. But instead of making a strong public case for better designed policies—policies predicated on the belief that both environmental protection and the protection of economic prosperity can actually go hand in hand—the party leadership has too often chosen to highlight the interests of the antiregulation lobby. As a result, as Republican pollster Frank Luntz pointed out in early 2003, "The environment is probably the single issue on which the Republicans . . . are most vulnerable."

It doesn't have to be this way. Protecting America's environment for future generations is just too important for this kind of extreme division to continue. Due in great part to the work of environmental groups and government, we have made remarkable progress over the past thirty-five years—our air is cleaner, our water purer, and our land better protected than it was. Much more remains to be done, but the impact of thirty-five years of the environmental movement has created a far more responsible environmental ethos in every part of our society. We are in a better position today than ever before to harness the ingenuity of American business and industry. Though some businesses are dragging their heels, many others have been won over. Hundreds of companies have seen the benefits, both to their reputations and their bottom lines, of acting as responsible environmental stewards.

One of the many responsible companies I saw firsthand was a BMW plant in South Carolina that was tapping into methane gas produced by a nearby landfill for 25 percent of its energy needs, reducing carbon dioxide emissions at that one facility by about fifty-five thousand tons a year. When I visited that plant in April 2003, they were just getting started. A year later, plant officials reported that the project had "exceeded expectations," had saved BMW more than a million dollars in energy costs, and had helped inspire similar efforts elsewhere in the state. But there was more: a South Carolina state energy official said that BMW's efforts at that plant had "raised the awareness of landfill gas to energy all over the world." Such is the power of a good example coupled with a positive contribution to the bottom line.

The old methods of "command and control" from Washington, although appropriate when they were enacted, are no longer the only way to meet the next generation of environmental challenges. We can make more headway by engaging proactively in preventing pollution than if we simply wait to find the bad actors that are already polluting and seek to punish them. And although the environment is cleaner and healthier now than it was thirty-five years ago, we still face significant challenges, including rising rates of childhood asthma, an aging drinking-water infrastructure, high levels of mercury in our fish, pollution from power plants, and hundreds of Superfund sites still not cleaned up even as the Superfund Trust Fund runs out of money, to name just a few. The longer we delay, the harder and costlier the solutions will be.

When I accepted President Bush's invitation to join his administration at the EPA, I knew the president shared my vision of finding new, innovative ways to advance environmental goals—approaches that didn't rely on the heavy hand of government but would instead build partnerships around shared goals for a better environment. As governors, we knew that the states, as well as responsible businesses, could often find better, cheaper, faster ways of meeting tough federal standards if they were given that chance. I wanted to help advance such efforts at the national level.

The Bush administration deserves credit for some important environmental measures, including, among others, mandating major reductions in emissions from nonroad diesel engines, enacting legislation to accelerate the cleanup of thousands of polluted sites around the nation, committing to increasing wetlands in the United States, and tackling mercury emissions from power plants. It has also made important progress in promoting compliance with existing laws through incentives for responsible action that even exceeds federal standards. Through such programs as EPA's National Environmental Performance Track, companies that meet a higher level of compliance receive recognition for their responsible behavior, and their facilities are placed on low-inspection priority status, saving them the time and money other companies have to spend to prepare for and respond to inspection requests.

Unfortunately, our efforts in this direction, which have produced some impressive results, have been overshadowed by those in the administration, and in key leadership roles in the Congress, who never seem to miss an opportunity to dismiss environmental protection as a priority. When, for example, the White House declined to meet with representatives of the environmental groups regarding the work of the Energy Task Force while business was purported to have an open door, that approach only provided an opportunity for the Democrats and the environmental lobby to attack.

I arrived at the EPA optimistic that we could reach out effectively across the aisle and to the professional environmental lobby to make some substantial progress in areas such as clean air, toxic cleanup, and clean water. That optimism soon faded as I got my first dose of the political poison in Washington's world of environmental politics, and it tasted like arsenic.

While the presidential election of 2000 was still being decided, the Clinton administration was working around the clock to produce a last-minute flurry of new environmental regulations. When I arrived at my office for my first day of work, I found more than sixty different regulations moving forward—with some of them having been completed just days before the reins of power were turned over to the new administration. Among those regulations was a ticking time bomb—a new regulation about the acceptable levels of arsenic in drinking water.

It is customary for a new administration to review the eleventh-hour actions of its predecessor—just as it is common practice for a departing administration to cram as much into its final days as is humanly possible. Ironically, the final days of an administration may be some of its most productive, as those who are about to leave office seek to do all kinds of things they'd been unable—or unwilling—to complete during the previous four or eight years. Given the attention being paid to the president-elect at this time, a lame-duck president can often push measures through that would have been too controversial or politically difficult when people were still paying attention to him.

So it was no surprise when one of the first directives President Bush issued to his cabinet was a memo from the new White House chief of staff, Andy Card, instructing all cabinet members and agency heads to review that flurry of last-minute Clinton actions. This was standard operating procedure—similar memos had been issued at the beginning of several previous administrations—so when I directed the EPA staff to begin reviewing the many regulations my predecessor Carol Browner had left behind, they knew exactly how to proceed.

The vast majority of these new measures raised no concern, and we let them move forward without making any changes. A few, however, caught our attention—and one of those would end up grabbing the attention of people not just in the EPA, but all over the country.

Just three days before leaving office, the Clinton administration had proposed lowering the acceptable level of arsenic in public drinking water supplies from 50 parts per billion (ppb) to just 10, and it gave water companies until 2006 to meet the new standard. On its face, the new mandate seemed like a clear winner (as governor, I had lowered our state's drinking water standard for arsenic to 10 ppb). I knew from experience, however, that such a substantial change in a regulation can sometimes have unexpected negative consequences and must be carefully reviewed. The existing level had been in effect for almost sixty years, and though the Clinton administration had had eight years to do something about it, it was only in its waning hours that the lower level was proposed. So I asked for more information on the rationale behind the decision as well as information about the cost implications for water companies and their customers.

EPA career staff were confident that the current level of 50 ppb was too high, but they acknowledged that they hadn't had enough time to perform a thorough analysis of the impact of the change on those who would have to implement it. Specifically, they had not fully calculated, to my satisfaction, whether meeting the new standard would be affordable for the five thousand small water companies located in those parts of the country (mostly in the Southwest) where arsenic occurs naturally in ground water supplies.

I wanted to avoid what had happened in New River, Arizona, where the local water company shut down because the cost of upgrading its treatment system to meet the 50 ppb standard was too high. As a result, local residents had had to drill their own private wells (not subject to EPA safe drinking-water regulations), which registered levels of arsenic that were far above what the local utility's water had contained. Consequently, many New River residents now have to travel to a neighboring town to buy bottled water, while others are ingesting larger amounts of arsenic in their drinking water than they had before.

If we were going to take more time to evaluate the proposed new regulation, I had to act fast because the new standard would become official in just a matter of days. I reasoned that putting off the measure for a short period to assess its impact more fully would do no harm because the standard would not actually have to be met until 2006. Even a delay of a few months would still allow plenty of time for affected water companies to make any changes required. We would end up lowering the standard, but I wanted to be sure it was lowered to the right amount and in the right time frame. So after discussion with my senior staff and giving the White House a heads-up, on March 20, 2001, I put a hold on the regulation.

I'd had enough experience with the hard knocks of environmental politics to know that in announcing this decision, we had to do a thorough job explaining why we were taking extra time, and we had to emphasize that there was no doubt that we would end up lowering the standard—and I tried. But the environmental lobby, and the Democrats who were still infuriated by the election outcome, had no interest in acknowledging such subtleties.

I was frankly stunned by the firestorm this decision ignited. Rather than get any credit for a sincere effort to get a new regulation right, the administration's political enemies pounced. My decision was perceived as a golden opportunity to portray the president as an enemy of the environment. In this case, they charged he was acting as a tool of the mining industry, which environmentalists claimed would benefit if the standard wasn't lowered. Mining activity can disturb naturally occurring arsenic, potentially contaminating water supplies, which the mining companies might then have to pay to clean up, but that issue never came up in my discussions with staff.

One of the first salvos came from Senator Joe Lieberman, who had just lost the vice presidency in the closest election in more than a hundred years. He said my arsenic decision, "threaten[ed] to roll us right back to the Stone Age." His Senate colleague California's Barbara Boxer exclaimed that we had "declared war on the environment." The Natural Resources Defense Council asserted my decision would "force millions of Americans to continue to drink arsenic-laced water" and went on to claim that "many will die from arsenic-related cancers and other diseases but George Bush apparently doesn't care." A Philadelphia paper ran an editorial titled "OK Kids, Drink Up Your Daily Requirements of Arsenic," and a Georgia newspaper inaccurately headlined its news story EPA TO ALLOW MORE ARSENIC IN WATER.

I found these attacks absolutely outrageous, well beyond the bounds of typical partisan rhetoric. We weren't forcing anyone to drink arsenic-laced water, we weren't rolling back existing regulations, and we most certainly were not raising the acceptable levels and urging kids to increase their intake of arsenic. Yet the truth was no match for the vitriol we had unleashed.

The Democratic National Committee struck what was probably the lowest blow when it aired a television ad that pictured a cute little girl facing the camera and holding out a glass of water, saying, "May I please have some more arsenic in my water, Mommy?" The DNC had to know that the facts did not even remotely support the premise of their ad—but it was effective. Even today, I get asked why I wanted to put arsenic into America's drinking water.

In the end, after receiving the advice of the National Academy of Sciences and after securing money to develop technology to find more affordable methods of removing arsenic from water supplies (we also later found money to help small water systems meet the new standard), we lowered the standard to exactly where it had been proposed, to 10 ppb; and we made it effective in 2006, exactly when it was first proposed. That didn't stop Democrats from continuing to assert that the Bush administration favored putting arsenic into America's water supply. Six months after we set the new limit, Al Gore claimed, "They had a proposal to increase the levels that would be permitted." A year later, Bill Clinton said, Republicans "tried to put more arsenic in the water." And even as late as 2004, Dick Gephardt, then pursuing his third failed campaign for the Democratic presidential nomination, used the exact same language Clinton had used months earlier to claim in a debate that we "tried to put more arsenic in the water." *Slate* magazine condemned that remark as the "worst slander" in the debate. Apparently, once the political well was poisoned, there was no cleaning it up.

As much as I resented these attacks, I did take some comfort when in July 2004, Nebraska's senator Ben Nelson, a Democrat, introduced legislation to delay implementation of the new arsenic standard for small water companies because of the cost. As the Associated Press reported, " 'Imposing the new standards on such towns would force residents to dig private wells,' he said. 'They'd be drinking the same water. . . . It would absolutely disguise the problem—if there is, in fact, a problem.' "

That was my first, but certainly not my last, experience with the extent to which the partisan warfare over environmental issues has become disingenuous and extremist. Just how intent the environmental groups were on denying any positive environmental press for the Bush administration was brought home to me in an extraordinary series of events in 2003, not long before I left my post at the EPA.

Early in my tenure, we had okayed a regulation that had been drafted by the Clinton administration to reduce the amount of sulfur burned by diesel trucks and on-road vehicles. We then went a step further. Nonroad diesel engines, such as tractors and backhoes, had never been regulated, even though they posed an even greater threat to air quality and public health than on-road diesels. To address that glaring problem, I instructed the EPA staff to develop a proposal to require cleaner diesel engines for off-road equipment.

I faced some initial skepticism in the agency, both among career staff and political appointees, about our ability to get such a regulation past the White House. Many assumed that because farmers and the construction industry were important to the president's political base, we would face insurmountable opposition. Those assumptions were not borne out. Before I left the agency, the White House approved our proposed new regulation to require mandatory reduction in nonroad diesel emissions by 90 percent, preventing more than fourteen thousand premature deaths every year, and we published them in the Federal Register. Several months later, these new regulations were made final, without any substantive changes.

Working with both engine manufacturers and environmentalists, we had been able to craft a proposal that received support from both sectors. That was precisely the kind of constructive work on significant new measures that I had believed we could achieve with the right approach. Indeed, when we unveiled the regulation, the National Resources Defense Council (NRDC), one of the largest environmental lobbies in the country, proclaimed that our proposal " . . . will be the biggest public health step since lead was removed from gasoline more than two decades ago." I was pleased that we'd shown that business and environmentalists could work together and that the pursuit of environmental progress and economic prosperity were not mutually exclusive goals.

Just three days later, however, the *Washington Post* reported that "other enviro groups were apoplectic" at the NRDC's statement, and were worried that it "would cripple environmentalists' efforts to criticize the administration's overall, far-from-perfect record." The article went on to quote an NRDC official as expressing "fear that 'Karl Rove is going to grab that quote and use it the way a producer uses an out-of-context quote in a review of a bad play.' "

As a result, shortly after this story ran, the NRDC wrote me again, this time asking me to stop quoting their statement of support. And we wonder why we can't make progress!

Unfortunately, extremism and closed-mindedness have been all too prevalent in certain powerful quarters on the other side in recent years, too. The American Chemistry Council fought hard against my efforts to require certain high-risk chemical plants to assess and address their vulnerability to terrorist attacks after September 11. Numerous businesses and trade associations, often represented by powerful Republicans, spend millions of dollars each year lobbying against virtually any new environmental regulation, invariably claiming it will hamstring their ability to stay in business, even though a great many American companies have figured out that good environmental practices are also good business practices. Many others, however, almost reflexively oppose any mandate to improve their environmental performance, no matter how much it needs improving. I sometimes wonder whether those companies spend more money trying to defeat new regulations than they would by simply complying with them.

And they have their supporters in the GOP, some of whom are well placed to thwart progress. The chairman of the Senate environment committee, Jim Inhofe of Oklahoma, and his counterpart on the House side while I was at the EPA, Representative Billy Tauzin, both used their positions to bottleneck some important environmental proposals. One notable and unfortunate example was their opposition, in the months following 9/11, to giving EPA much-needed regulatory authority to require thousands of chemical facilities around the nation to assess and address their vulnerability to terrorist attack.

In 2002, the National Strategy for Homeland Security gave EPA the federal lead for protecting the nation's chemical facilities. As part of our effort to help carry out that duty, my staff and I worked closely with Tom Ridge and his staff at the White House Office of Homeland Security (this was prior to the creation of the Department of Homeland Security) to draft legislation that would require just a fraction of the nation's half a million chemical sites (the fifteen thousand that had the greatest amount of toxic chemicals located near large populations centers) to undertake vulnerability assessments, take reasonable steps to address those vulnerabilities, and report to the EPA that they had complied.

Although both Tom and I agreed such legislation was necessary, strong congressional opposition—led by some Republicans on the Senate Environment and Public Works Committee and the House Energy and Commerce Committee—to giving EPA even this modest additional statutory authority made it difficult to secure administration support for a meaningful bill. I finally grew so frustrated with the lack of support we were receiving in meeting our responsibility, I formally asked the White House's Office of Homeland Security to relieve EPA of its lead responsibility for reducing the vulnerability of the chemical sector to attack. I did not believe the agency should be asked to assume responsibility for performing this important mission if it would not also be given even the basic authority it needed to meet it.

As a matter of principle, Republicans have long been the major advocates of less rather than more government regulation. That's a principle I share. In the past, however, the party has been willing to make sensible compromises in order to address the many serious threats to the environment. Even the most anti-Washington Republicans recognized that when rivers were spontaneously combusting (as the Cuyahoga River in Cleveland did in 1969), and when fish you caught in a local river or lake couldn't be safely served to your family (a problem that still exists), drastic and immediate action was called for. As much as federal regulation may have gone against their usual thinking, Republicans at the beginning of the modern environmental movement saw the need and acted. The first administrator of the EPA, Bill Ruckelshaus, in talking about the early days of the EPA, once recalled, "[President] Nixon would react negatively to anything that smacked of regulation, that would interfere with the economy." That's a natural Republican reaction, but it didn't stop Nixon, or his Republican successors, from moving aggressively to meet the environmental challenges America faced.

That's not to say that I don't understand the frustrations so many Republicans feel with the present state of our environmental regulations. There's no doubt that the command-and-control approach to environmental protection, which was absolutely appropriate and necessary when EPA was established by President Nixon in 1970, led to some excesses.

In the 1980s, EPA came under considerable criticism for the way it handled the entire issue surrounding asbestos in public schools. Following enactment of the Asbestos Hazard Emergency Response Act in 1986, which EPA was responsible for enforcing, billions of dollars were spent by school districts around the nation removing asbestos from their school buildings, even when the asbestos was in good condition and was not releasing fibers into the air. The high costs of removals, coupled with anecdotal reports that some removal efforts actually resulted in higher levels of airborne asbestos fibers, damaged the credibility of the agency. Today, the EPA advises that most asbestos in school buildings can be "managed properly where it is" and that "removal is generally necessary only when the [asbestos-containing] material damage is extensive and severe." Controversies such as this have only fed the appetite of those who are eager to trim EPA's sails.

For thirty-five years, successful environmental policy making has been defined by using the wrong measures: the number of new laws passed, additional regulations promulgated, and by the amount of fines and fees collected. Politicians seeking to burnish their environmental reputations would talk about how many environmental bills they had introduced or how many polluters they had put out of business. That might have been appropriate at a time when we had so few regulations on the books, but at this point we should be more sophisticated in measuring our progress. We should be measuring success and determining whether the policies we've pursued have made America's air cleaner, its water purer, its land better protected, and its people healthier—these are after all, standards that really count. All the well-intended laws on the books wouldn't be worth much if they didn't produce results—and it's time we start judging success by measuring results. The people who criticize my environmental record in New Jersey point to modest reductions we made in the size of our environmental bureaucracy. They ignore the fact that the policies we put in place actually led to cleaner air, water, and land.

It's easier, of course, to measure the former than the latter. At my confirmation hearing, I told the senators about my plans to produce an environmental report card to measure what progress we had made over the previous thirty years. I later learned that my proposal had caused real consternation among career staff at the agency—something like that had never been tried before, and they were concerned I had made a promise we wouldn't be able to keep. In the end, it took two and a half years for the scientists from more than two dozen government departments and agencies, as well as from the National Academy of Sciences and several academic institutions, to agree on how to measure our environmental progress (no wonder it hadn't been done before). Just before I left the EPA, however, we were able to release the first State of the Environment Report, which showed that while we have made significant progress, there's more work to do. At least now we have standards with which to measure and benchmarks against which to evaluate future progress.

Although I share the frustration so many Republicans feel over the excessive emphasis on writing even more regulations, and on the tactic the environmentalists use of refusing to recognize the progress we've made, the problem is that too many Republicans these days (especially those in leadership posts in Washington) often go to the opposite extreme—denying that the environment needs any additional legal and regulatory protection and seeking to roll back some regulations that have done so much good. All too often, the leadership of the party has chosen to play to the interests of the antiregulation element of the base while seeking to redress the legitimate concern that all balance has been lost in the making and enforcement of environmental policy and regulations.

Rather than forcefully and consistently making the case for more innovative environmental policies, the approach in recent years has always been to emphasize instead the party's sympathy with the concerns of business. This was made abundantly clear to me very early on in my tenure at EPA with respect to the issue of global climate change (or global warming) when the administration abruptly reversed itself in a way that would have serious consequences.

Less than six weeks after I began working at EPA, I was scheduled to travel to Trieste, Italy, for what would be my first meeting with my G8 counterparts—the environmental ministers from Canada, Britain, France, Germany, Japan, Italy, and Russia. Since this was my first international trip representing the United States government—and knowing a second chance to make a good first impression is never possible—I began preparing for it as soon as I arrived at the agency.

The official purpose of the meeting was to further an ongoing effort among the G8 to agree on the next steps in addressing global warming. This meeting was in preparation for a highly anticipated much larger international meeting to be held in 2002 in Johannesburg. I was keenly aware that this preparatory meeting was the first opportunity for our closest allies to take the measure of President Bush's stance on environmental policies. I also knew their expectations were low because of the rhetoric of the presidential campaign and the fact that the president had come out against U.S. ratification of the Kyoto Protocol before the 2000 election. This controversial international treaty—which, at the time, had been ratified by only one industrial country, Romania—requires much of the developed world to make significant reductions in greenhouse gas emissions (such as carbon dioxide emissions from cars and power-generating facilities) in an effort to slow global warming.

There has never been much support in the United States in either party for ratifying Kyoto. It was seen as fatally flawed, largely because it didn't apply to nations such as China and India, which, along with the rest of Asia, are expected to account for as much as 70 percent of the global growth in greenhouse gases over the next fifteen years. There was also considerable skepticism about the ability of any developed nation to meet the aggressive goals the treaty set forth along with concern about the economic costs of even trying. For these reasons, in 1997, the U.S. Senate (including John Kerry) had voted 95 to 0 to oppose the provisions of the treaty. Following that, Congress included specific provisions in numerous appropriations bills prohibiting the expenditure of any federal government funds on any activities that would implement the provisions of the treaty. Recognizing political reality, the Clinton administration, a strong advocate of the Protocol, never even sent it to the Senate for ratification.

As governor, I had made clear my opposition to ratification of the Kyoto Protocol for the reasons cited above. At the same time, however, I felt we had a responsibility to begin to reduce greenhouse gases in my state. In 1998 we established an initiative in New Jersey to reduce greenhouse gas emissions 3.5 percent below 1990 levels by 2005. I strongly believed then, as I do now, that the United States should commit itself to reducing its greenhouse gas emissions, a goal President Bush also supports.

During the 2000 campaign, candidate Bush made clear his opposition to the treaty itself, but he also argued that the United States should work with other countries to develop new technologies to reduce harmful emissions. He had even expressed support for legislation to require the mandatory reduction in the United States of emissions of sulfur dioxide, nitrogen oxide, mercury, and the major greenhouse gas, carbon dioxide, from power plants. Although it was little noticed at the time, his inclusion of carbon dioxide in his proposal was significant. Many Republicans had been arguing for years that carbon dioxide was not a pollutant, and they were bound to oppose any effort to regulate it, as was much of the utility industry. However, a mandatory cap on carbon dioxide emissions was listed as one of the Bush campaign's promises in the thick notebook titled "Transition 2001," a copy of which I was given when I was nominated for the EPA position. That notebook was the official compendium of the president's campaign promises, written by the Bush-Cheney transition team (which was chaired by the vice president-elect).

The U.S. refusal to ratify Kyoto had riled our allies in the G8 and most everyone else in the global community. Although polls show very little concern in the United States about global climate change, most of the rest of the world sees this as the world's most important environmental issue. International resentment against the United States (which is both the world's largest economy and the world's largest producer of greenhouse gases) for its decision not to ratify had been simmering for some time. So before the Trieste meeting, I knew I would face tough challenges on this issue from the other environmental ministers. I believed, however, that the president's support for emissions controls—especially for a cap on carbon dioxide emissions—would allow me to get our discussions off on a positive, productive foot.

Shortly before leaving for Trieste, I met at the White House with Condi Rice, the president's National Security Adviser, and we went over the issues I expected to confront at the G8. I made sure she knew I would be touting the president's campaign commitment to a mandatory cap on carbon dioxide emissions, and she agreed that this was a sound approach. I also checked with the office of the White House chief of staff about the issue and got the green light from it as well.

Sure enough, at the meeting I confronted a good deal of skepticism about the administration's intentions on global climate change. One casual encounter in particular drove home just how strained our relations with our allies had become over this issue. I was walking across the square in the middle of Trieste late one afternoon between meetings, accompanied by the fairly large security detail the Italian government had insisted on providing. About halfway across the square I spotted David Anderson, Canada's environmental minister, coming toward us. I was struck by the fact that he was alone and I wondered how he had managed to shake his security detail. When we met up, I asked him right away, "David, where's your security?" He replied with a smile.

"I don't need any—no one hates Canada." That simple exchange reminded me of how much work we had to do in a hostile world, even with our allies, to convince them that we shared their concern over the state of the world.

Over the course of the meeting in Trieste, I assured my G8 counterparts that the president's campaign commitment to seek a mandatory cap on carbon dioxide emissions was solid and that the administration sincerely agreed that global climate change was a serious problem that demanded attention. By the end of the two-day meeting, we were all able to agree to language committing our respective countries to "[T]ake the lead by strengthening and implementing national programs and actions to reduce greenhouse gas emissions." In an article following the publication of that statement, the international news service Reuters reported, "Environmental activists said the statement was better than expected and that Christine Todd Whitman, head of the U.S. Environmental Protection Agency (EPA), had provided a clear and welcome signal to G-8 partners that Washington was serious about global warming." I was pleased that things had started off so well.

I also knew, though, that many Republicans in Congress, as well as many utility industry leaders, had already voiced their opposition to the president's promise to seek mandatory caps on carbon dioxide emissions. In fact, they had signaled behind the scenes that they would be perfectly happy to see the United States completely disengage from the rest of the international community on the climate change issue—which many of them thought was really just a hyped-up Trojan horse effort to use a false concern about a nonexistent problem to weaken U.S. economic strength. One economist's estimates best summed up their fear of having to comply with Kyoto: "GDP would decline by 4.2 percent, or $350 billion a year. . . . In human terms, this translates into the loss of 1.1 U.S. million jobs each year over a 15-year period." Although the economic impact of the treaty was a real and valid concern, such estimates cannot stand alone—they must also factor in the cost of doing nothing. So on the plane home, I wrote a memo to the president summarizing the trip, which I sent to him as soon as I arrived back in the United States.

In the memo, I emphasized several points that had been reinforced for me in Trieste. First, that the world community was very seriously concerned about climate change and was convinced of the need for immediate action. Second, that they believed that without the involvement of the United States, significant progress would be impossible. Third, that we were in a position to build some goodwill with our allies even without endorsing the specifics of Kyoto. Fourth, that expectations were low for the administration. I closed the memo with these words: "I would strongly recommend that you continue to recognize that global warming is a real and serious issue. While not specifically endorsing the targets called for in Kyoto, you could indicate that you are exploring how to reduce U.S. greenhouse gas emissions internally and will continue to do so no matter what else transpires." I concluded, "Mr. President, this is a credibility issue (global warming) for the U.S. in the international community. It is also an issue that is resonating here at home. We need to appear engaged and shift the discussion from the focus on the 'K' word to action, but we have to build some bona fides first."

Unfortunately, as I was to learn later, before I had even boarded the plane to come home, an effort was being launched by key Republican members of Congress and energy industry leaders to persuade the president to strengthen his opposition to Kyoto by reversing himself on his commitment to a carbon dioxide cap. Before I had left for Italy, the White House office of legislative affairs had started to hear complaints about statements I had made in an interview on CNN regarding the president's support for a carbon dioxide emissions cap, and the administration had begun a review of the campaign promise. Once I repeated those statements at the G8, those opposing that proposal had shifted into high gear. While I was writing my memo to the president, four Republican senators—Chuck Hagel of Nebraska, Jesse Helms of North Carolina, Larry Craig of Idaho, and Pat Roberts of Kansas—were writing a letter of their own to him, expressing their strong opposition to his campaign promise on carbon emissions. They made clear, in no uncertain terms, that they thought the commitment was bad policy and bad politics and that they would vigorously oppose any such measure if the president were to actually propose it. That letter apparently accelerated the White House review of the carbon dioxide cap promise, and within the week after I had returned from Trieste, EPA staff had been called to numerous White House meetings to discuss the issue.

From the reports I was getting back from staff, it had begun to look as if the president was indeed preparing to reverse his position—or, at the very least, that the White House staff, in concert with the vice president's office and senior staff from other departments, including the departments of Energy and Commerce, was preparing to recommend such a step, using the need to protect U.S. energy production as justification. Apparently, everyone in those meetings was using the California energy crisis to justify a reversal on the cap. Since half of the nation's energy needs are met by burning coal—the biggest producer of carbon dioxide emissions—they predicted a cap would reduce the availability and raise the cost of coal-generated power, at least in the short term. They saw the situation in California, with its rolling black-outs and frequent brownouts, as just the canary in the coal mine and asserted that the country's energy supply would be seriously disrupted unless the president reversed his position. My staff told me that theirs were the only voices in the room who strongly argued that the president's campaign promise be kept.

I knew the president was facing considerable pressure, but when the White House asked me to hold time early the follow-ing week to meet with the president on this issue, I thought I still had a fighting chance to make my case for keeping his pledge. The meeting was set for 10 A.M. on Tuesday, March 13, in the Oval Office. I spent the weekend preparing my arguments because I knew there would be no time for a long drawn-out discussion, and that the president wasn't inclined to hear one even had time allowed. But as soon as the president and I sat down, I realized that I wasn't there to state my case—I was there to be told that he had decided to reverse himself. He knew that his decision was leav-ing me out on a limb, and he apologized for that, and he did so again in front of the entire cabinet at its next meeting. He told me that he believed, however, that the looming national energy crisis made it unwise to impose any additional environmental bur-dens on utilities. I thought that rationale was too focused on the short term. I believed the president could keep his promise to cap carbon dioxide emissions, without threatening the energy supply, by phasing the mandatory reductions in over a period of years, enabling utilities to make whatever adjustments they needed to reduce their emissions without crippling their ability to meet the nation's energy needs. The White House didn't see it that way.

As I emerged from the Oval Office into the narrow hallway just outside it, I ran into Vice President Cheney. He was in his overcoat and was clearly in a hurry, as if late. He muttered a brief hello to me as he asked an aide who had come up behind me, "Do you have it?" The aide handed him a letter, which he tucked into his pocket as he rushed out, on his way to Capitol Hill for his weekly policy meeting with Republican senators.

As I would soon discover, the letter the vice president had stopped to pick up was the president's answer to the appeal sent by the Senator Hagel and his three colleagues the week before. In his reply, the president restated his opposition to the Kyoto Protocol, and then added, "I do not believe . . . that the government should impose on power plants mandatory emissions reductions for carbon dioxide, which is not a pollutant under the Clean Air Act." By stating that carbon dioxide was not a pollutant, he had issued an even stronger repudiation of his campaign position than Hagel and his allies on the Hill had expected.

Though I didn't know about the specific contents of the president's letter when I left the White House, I was well aware what the reaction would be once his decision on carbon was announced. As soon as I got into my car for the four-block ride back to EPA headquarters, I called my chief of staff, Eileen McGinnis, and asked her to gather the senior staff. We were going to have to fashion a response immediately because I knew that the

Democrats and the environmental lobby would have a field day with the reversal.

I knew my G8 environmental counterparts would not be pleased, to say the least. After all, the assurances I had given them just ten days before were now moot. They would feel deceived, which would make it even more difficult to deal with them on the many other international issues we would face. So as soon as I got back to my office, I placed calls to Ottawa, Mexico City, London, and several other capitals. I wanted them, at the least, to hear the news from me and not from press reports.

The first person I reached was David Anderson in Canada, who warned me that the decision was a mistake, and he predicted that it would have repercussions beyond this one area—a sentiment I would hear repeated as I made the calls. I felt those warnings were significant enough that later that day I called Secretary of State Colin Powell to discuss the issue with him. Colin immediately understood the impact this announcement would have on the international community. We discussed how important it was that the decision not be discussed in terms of the need to protect our own economy (which other nations would see as arrogant and dismissive), but rather on the need for a more effective mechanism for reducing carbon dioxide emissions worldwide.

Meanwhile, the White House and the conservative Republicans on the Hill had already come up with their spin on the decision: it was a victory for American independence from foreign intervention in the U.S. economy, and besides, as the Congress particularly felt, the greenhouse problem might not even be real. The Republican leadership was clearly aligning itself with those who chose to believe that global warming was little more than a convenient, and probably incorrect, theory advanced by those who wanted to weaken America's economy and its competitiveness in the world. The president's decision was meant to mollify the antiregulation element of the far-right base, and it was made with too little regard for what is in fact a serious problem, or for how it would be received by both moderates in the United States and our allies overseas.

The international reaction played out just as I'd expected. One London newspaper reflected what I was hearing, and would continue to hear from foreign governments in the years ahead, "At a single stroke, the United States has condemned the planet to a more polluted, less certain future. . . . Mr. Bush has made it clear he has concerns far more pressing than the health of the global environment. The country that emits 25 percent of the world's carbon dioxide with less than four percent of its population is not going to slow down."

Perhaps the ultimate irony in all this was that the president did truly believe that global climate change was a significant problem. Over the years, he has designated more money for research into the causes of global climate change and into developing technologies to reduce greenhouse gas emissions—including carbon dioxide—than any prior administration. The administration's insistence on playing strictly to the base in explaining the president's opposition to ratifying the Kyoto Protocol, coupled with his reversal on the regulation of carbon dioxide, was an early expression of the go-it-alone attitude that so offended our allies in the lead-up to the Iraq war. The roots of our difficulties in forging a strong multinational alliance to fight terrorism go all the way back to how we handled Kyoto as well as other international issues, including our participation in the International Criminal Court and the imposition of steel tariffs. I didn't disagree with the president's actions; I do believe we should have done a better job explaining them. Sometimes, as the old adage goes, it's not what you say, it's how you say it that's important.

In July 2004, British Prime Minister Tony Blair was under hostile questioning in the House of Commons about his close relationship with President Bush and the United States. In response, Blair felt compelled to point out that he disagreed with the president about the Kyoto Protocol, but he hoped that the United States would be willing to continue to talk about the need for global action on global climate change. "I do not think we should give up on dialogue with the United States," Blair told his skeptical colleagues. The fact that our closest international ally has to try to convince his own party members that they should not "give up" on the United States on what most of the world sees as the international community's most pressing issue should give one pause.

The immediate response from the Democrats and the environmental lobby was, of course, swift and withering. A leading House Democrat declared the president's decision, "a breathtaking betrayal," whereas the head of the National Environmental Trust said, "President Bush no longer has any credibility on environmental issues." The response went beyond the predictable partisan attacks. I recently read an analysis that showed that in the weeks following the president's letter to Senator Hagel, more than forty major newspapers wrote editorials (many for the first time) urging the United States to take steps to reduce greenhouse gas emissions.

Perhaps the only group that showed more energy in reacting to the president's decision than the Democrats and environmentalists was the hard-right wing of the Republican Party. Stung by the charge that the president had flip-flopped on this issue, they set out to demonstrate that he had never really supported a cap on carbon dioxide in the first place. The leader of this effort was columnist and frequent CNN talking head Bob Novak.

On numerous occasions on television and in print, Novak argued that I had ignited this controversy by taking one obscure reference to capping carbon dioxide emissions in a speech that the then governor Bush had given the previous fall in Michigan and creating policy out of it. "It was in the forty-ninth paragraph of a sixty-paragraph speech on energy. . . . Somebody slipped it in. But the left-wing activists at the Environmental Protection Agency noticed it. They fed it to Governor Whitman. She went on the air with it without checking with the White House, and if she's humiliated, she deserves it because this is a conservative administration and that kind of nonsense has no place in it," Novak sputtered on CNN's *Capital Gang* on March 17. Two days later, Novak ranted, "During the campaign, a line was slipped into a speech by Bush embracing the advanced ecoactivist position that emissions of carbon dioxide should be regulated. There was absolutely no discussion inside the campaign and no sense by anybody—including the news media—that a policy commitment had been reached. Five months later, Environmental Protection Administrator Christie Whitman picked up the line and exalted it, incorrectly, as Bush doctrine."

It seemed clear that Novak was hawking a line that could only have come from a source inside the White House who was eager to marginalize the emissions proposal (that suspicion was confirmed when the private memo I had written to the president on my way back from Italy was later leaked to the press). Of course Novak's assertion was dead wrong, as the carbon cap proposal had not only been included in a speech, it had also appeared on the campaign's Web site and was included in the transition team's "policy" notebook.

I recognize that, at the time, many of the president's political opponents were more than a bit disingenuous in attacking the president for abandoning the Protocol, when the previous administration never even sent it to the Senate for a vote. There's no doubt, however, that in foreign capitals—and around dinner tables in Britain, France, and Germany—people resented what they saw as our ready willingness to dismiss their concerns about the future of the planet and their economic futures in favor of our own.

Another example of the administration deciding to play to the antiregulation base rather than to aggressively push its own alternative approach to environmental policies is the failure of the president's Clear Skies initiative. In this case, even as we at the EPA were working with the White House on Clear Skies, the president's landmark proposal for mandatory controls of certain utility emissions, the Energy Task Force headed by Dick Cheney pushed for a different, and less comprehensive, reform of emissions controls that industry favored.

It's hard to remember now that the top domestic priority in the early months of the Bush administration was developing and then enacting the nation's first comprehensive energy policy in a generation. In early 2001, California was in the midst of a serious energy crisis. Rolling blackouts, accusations of market manipulation by energy wholesalers, and huge increases in energy costs were shaking California's economy. Many observers, and members of the administration, thought that California's energy crisis foreshadowed a coming national crisis. In response, just nine days after he took office, the president appointed Vice President Cheney to head the National Energy Policy Development Group (which became known as the Energy Task Force) to formulate policy recommendations, which would then make their way into the comprehensive energy plan the president would eventually propose in May 2001. I was appointed to serve on the task force, and the experience was an eye-opening encounter with just how obsessed so many of those in the energy industry, and in the Republican Party, have become with doing away with environmental regulation.

At our first meeting, I was somewhat taken aback to find that most of the members of the task force placed the blame for America's energy woes squarely on the nation's environmental laws and regulations. It had become conventional wisdom among many that California's energy problems were a direct result of excessive environmental regulations frustrating the efforts of utilities to increase capacity. As staff work on the Energy Task Force's report proceeded, it became clear that the overall tone of the report would seek to lay the blame for America's energy woes on America's environmental policies. At one meeting, after hearing one person after another lay the blame for our energy crisis squarely at EPA's door, I asked each of them to prepare a list of the energy projects that were being delayed because of environmental laws and regulations so I could fix the problem. Nobody ever did. (In the end, however, nearly half of the more than one hundred proposals contained in the energy plan promoted conservation, efficiency, and clean energy.)

Those who held this view identified the primary culprit of our energy crisis to be a complicated regulation known as New Source Review (NSR), which the EPA was responsible for enforcing. Some wanted to reform it; others wanted to do away with NSR entirely.

NSR is a classic example of good intentions resulting in questionable policy. When the Clear Air Act was originally enacted, it required new power plants to include modern air pollution control technology, but it exempted existing plants from having to add the controls, allowing them to perform "routine repair and maintenance" of their facilities without triggering the provisions of the act. The assumption was that aging plants would eventually be replaced by new facilities, which would have to comply. It soon became apparent, however, that some utilities were increasing the capacity of their old plants, and thus their emissions, while describing the changes as mere "routine repair and replacement." As a result, EPA decided to require utilities to seek agency review of their "routine" changes to determine if they resulted in such new sources of emissions into the air (hence, New Source Review). Unfortunately, however, no one had ever clearly defined "routine," and with the regulation being so unclearly written, the EPA never made a concerted effort to enforce NSR on power plants.

That changed when the Clinton administration, during its second term, decided to begin using NSR to file numerous multimillion-dollar lawsuits against electric utilities, charging that they had evaded the law in the past and now had to pay the consequences. The flurry of lawsuits not only angered power companies, it also provoked the ire of many of those Republicans on Capitol Hill who almost always opposed any increase in the regulatory reach of the EPA. People became focused on reforming NSR, with some intent on getting rid of it altogether. The vice president seemed particularly eager about the issue, and he called me on several occasions, even tracking me down when I was on vacation in Colorado, to press his view that NSR reform should be part of the national energy plan on which the Energy Task Force was working.

The criticisms of NSR surely had some merit, and especially the criticisms of the sudden decision by the Clinton administration to pursue lawsuits—after more than five years in office. Some utilities had clearly violated the intent of the regulation. Because "routine repair and maintenance" had never been defined, compliance was open to confusion. Clarifying that language would have been a much more reasonable first step. (Interestingly, the Clinton administration had attempted to craft a definition, but they were never able to reach an internal consensus.)

Numerous voices were calling for a change, including the National Governors Association, which had passed a unanimous resolution calling for NSR reform. Although I agreed that there was a real need for the reform, I did not support doing it in the context of the Energy Task Force. I believed strongly that NSR reform was first and foremost an environmental issue, which should not be part of the task force's work. Because the Clear Skies Bill I was working on with the White House would have eliminated NSR, I made the case with the Energy Task Force for taking NSR reform out of the national energy plan. Instead, I pushed for using the elimination of NSR as a carrot to help build support for Clear Skies. After all, if the power industry really wanted to reform—or even eliminate—NSR, why would it not use that desire to help the president get what he wanted—Clear Skies. I was convinced that if the administration was serious about Clear Skies, it would use that leverage to win support for Clear Skies. I took this argument to many in the White House, including the president and vice president, but I didn't get far.

The push to reform NSR by Republican congressional members and industry leaders was so strong that the task force continued to press the case, and at one point, even considered giving the Department of Energy the responsibility for NSR reform, since, in their mind, NSR was really an issue of energy production, not environmental protection. I was able to successfully beat that suggestion back, and in the end, EPA retained control of NSR reform (although the White House maintained an active role in determining what reform ultimately looked like). The agency's recommendations didn't move forward until after I had left it. I had, however, signed initial reforms to NSR (which were aimed primarily at manufacturing plants and didn't affect utilities in any meaningful way). The major reforms were proposed after I had left the agency. I must say that I'm glad they weren't able to finish the work until after I was home in New Jersey. I could not have signed regulatory changes that would have undermined the environmentally important NSR cases that were working their way through the courts.

The most frustrating aspect of the NSR debate was that the ardent antiregulation Republican voices had shown so little regard for the passage of Clear Skies, a bill the president himself unveiled on February 12, 2002. Clear Skies would have required a mandatory 70 percent reduction in power plant emissions of nitrogen oxides, sulfur dioxide, and mercury, making it the most ambitious air quality plan ever proposed by any president. It also would have made NSR obsolete, because it would have eliminated the distinction between new plants, old plants, and modifications to old plants. The entire industry would have been required to reduce their emissions, in whatever ways they decided worked best for them. How better to reform NSR than by eliminating it?

Clear Skies was modeled after the highly successful cap-and-trade approach to reduce acid rain that was part of the Clean Air Act Amendments of 1990, signed into law by the first President Bush in 1990. That bill achieved greater reductions in acid rain faster and less expensively than anyone expected. This approach gave industry exactly what it had always said it wanted—clear standards, certainty, and flexibility in meeting environmental goals, no matter how tough they were. The industry has long maintained it wasn't against cleaner air; it just was against government telling it exactly how to achieve that goal. I knew there was merit to that argument because I had seen in New Jersey that when we gave manufacturing plants flexibility in meeting tough, comprehensive environmental standards, they either met them or we fined them. More often than not, they met them.

The support I had hoped would form behind Clear Skies never materialized, and the fact that we didn't have NSR reform to use as leverage surely didn't help. I had been well aware that getting Clear Skies through Congress would be a real battle. When I placed a courtesy call to Congressman John Dingell, the ranking

Democrat on the House Energy and Commerce Committee, to tell him that we were going to introduce the bill, he told me in no uncertain terms that I didn't know what I was getting myself in for and would come to regret it. He still had the scars from the long and drawn-out fight over previous efforts to modify the Clean Air Act, he said, and he didn't believe that we could get anything through. Although I respected his experience, I also knew that the president was for the bill, and I believed that with an all-out push from the White House we had a chance. Unfortunately, that was not to be. Outside the EPA, there was not much commitment by the administration to Clear Skies. A recent search of the White House Web site reveals that the president has only mentioned Clear Skies nine times in the nearly three years since it was introduced—and six of those times were during Earth Day commemorations.

The Democratic Party and environmental groups were of no help either. Rather than appreciating what a substantial step forward in emissions control Clear Skies would have been, and supporting the bill but negotiating about the specifics—such as asking, "Is 70 percent the best we can do; can we raise the amount of the reductions or accelerate the timetable for achieving them?"—the Democrats and the environmental lobby characterized the bill as a retreat from environmental protection because it did not include regulations on carbon dioxide. The Green Group meeting I recounted earlier was just one of many times when I heard people who claim to care about the environment tell me they'd rather see no bill enacted than see Clear Skies, even if amended, become law.

Surely the best way to make major improvements to the quality of America's air is by adding clear and unambiguous mandatory pollution reductions to the Clean Air Act. If you pass legislation clearly defining the amount of pollution reductions needed, it becomes the law. It's not subject to endless interpretation and legal challenges the way regulations often are. That is why Clear Skies makes sense and why the stubborn ideological antiregulation mind-set of many Republicans, and the equally stubborn position of environmentalists about the carbon dioxide issue and, it must be said, the desire of the Democrats to prevent the administration from claiming any environmental victories, resulted in a stalemate. The losers are the American people and our environment.

I believe that the intransigence on both extremes of the environmental debate is preventing significant progress that might be made if there was less fixation on doing away with all regulations on one side and with writing more and more regulations on the other, and that a more sincere effort is needed to promote positive economic incentives for businesses to make improvements. As we saw under the Clean Air Act Amendments of 1990 and its success in reducing acid rain, policies that reward early compliance and provide flexibility in how business meets tough environmental standards can produce real results. Such efforts allow businesses to remain economically competitive without sacrificing our continued advancement toward a cleaner environment and a healthier society.

I found that that promoting compliance and prevention produced good success when I implemented such policies in New Jersey. I also found that the all-too-popular notion—among both Republicans and Democrats—that environmental progress is necessarily at odds with business interests is just plain wrong. When I took office as governor in 1994, both New Jersey's environment and its economy were suffering. During the year before I took office, the state registered unhealthy ozone levels in the air on an average of once every six days, and New Jersey's industrial facilities were pumping nearly seventeen million pounds of waste into the environment each year. Beaches along New Jersey's 127-mile-long coastline were closed more than thirty times for exceeding safe bacteria levels that year. Open space and farmland were being gobbled up by development at a rate that threatened to permanently degrade the state's quality of life.

New Jersey's economy wasn't in much better shape. Over the previous four years, the state had lost 450,000 jobs, unemployment had reached all-time highs, taxes were skyrocketing, and employers were leaving the state in droves. Although the entire region was experiencing an economic slowdown, New Jersey's economy lagged far behind those of our neighboring states.

Many in the business community claimed that part of the problem lay in the impact of what they saw as excessive environmental regulation and overzealous enforcement. Although I couldn't fully credit that explanation, I did have to question why our Department of Environmental Protection (DEP) was so reliant on the fines, fees, and penalties it collected for its funding. As one New Jersey–based international business consultant put it, "DEP [is allowed] to raise fines and fees to ridiculous levels and keep that money. . . . All the department is interested in is the revenue. It has nothing to do with protecting the environment."

That may have been an overstatement, but I did believe that making the department rely on fees and fines for the bulk of its budget provided exactly the wrong incentive—it encouraged the DEP regulators to fine first and ask questions later. I believed we should work to prevent pollution before it starts, and the best way to do that was to remove the incentive for levying heavy fines and instead provide incentives to encourage positive behavior. The first step was to fund the DEP out of general revenues.

I also couldn't understand why the state of New Jersey had an environmental department larger than that of the state of California, which is twenty-two times the area of New Jersey. To me this was evidence of a bureaucracy that had grown out of control. So I proposed a modest cut in both the department's annual funding and in its overall staffing level. From the reaction this proposal unleashed, you'd have I thought I had proposed abolishing the entire department.

My plan was greeted by immediate howls of protest from Democrats and environmentalists. One Democratic state senator accused me of being "relentlessly against strong environmental protection." A group of environmental lobbyists called me a "polluter's dream," and claimed that I was "leading the attack on the environment." They spent a hundred thousand dollars to buy radio ads attacking my efforts as "a disaster."

Nevertheless, we moved forward and made the changes I proposed. In time, the size of the DEP was reduced (although only by a modest 2 percent) and the department was brought on budget. Most important, the state's economy came roaring back, and the condition of the environment improved significantly. During my last year as governor, the number of unhealthy ozone days had been cut to just four for the year, beach closings had been reduced to just eleven over the course of the summer. The amount of industrial pollution emitted into the environment had been cut by nearly 60 percent (a decrease of eight millions pounds a year), and we had preserved more open space and farmland than under all previous administrations combined, while also putting in place a plan (and the funding) to preserve one million acres more of open space and farmland over the following decade.

During my seven years as governor, I spent a great deal of time promoting the new approach we were taking to protect the environment—moving away from measuring the strength of the state's commitment by tallying the number of fines, fees, regulations, and bureaucrats, to actually measuring the condition of the environment itself. Effecting these changes didn't require magic, just a consistent commitment to the goal. I regularly talked about common sense in environmental policy making, and I made the case clearly and consistently that environmental progress and economic prosperity are not mutually exclusive goals. I had a feeling I was making progress when, almost halfway through my first term, I read an article in the *Philadelphia Inquirer* that began, "When Gov. Whitman took office last year, environmentalists feared her pro-business agenda to stimulate jobs and economic growth would lead to a slash and burn policy toward the environment. But nearly two years into her first term, Whitman is neither as hostile to some of the goals of environmentalists—nor as friendly to business—as many anticipated when she took office. . . . That has created some grumbling among members of the business community." I took that as a sign we were following the proper course. You're probably on the right track if neither side feels it's getting everything it wants.

After I had served almost two years at the EPA, *Washington*

Post columnist Anne Applebaum wrote a piece titled "The EPA's Lonely Moderate." She recounted some of the battles I'd faced (and battle scars I'd received) in my effort to steer America's environmental policy on a sensible commonsense course. She began the last paragraph of her piece by asking, "[W]hether the intermediate position Whitman has carved out is a real one, with real political backing in the rest of her party and the rest of the administration, or whether she merely serves as window dressing for people who have other priorities but don't want to say so out loud." She then closed by asserting that my "success, or failure, will tell us whether compromise on the environment is even possible anymore."

After spending two and a half years at the EPA, I believe more strongly than ever that a progressive, results-oriented approach is needed in environmental policy making in the United States today. What's more, I believe it's time for the American people to demand an end to the extreme approaches taken by those on all sides of this debate. We are not on the verge of an environmental collapse that can be averted only if we shut down America's industries and turn our backs on continued economic progress. Nor is America's continued prosperity threatened by a maze of unintelligible environmental laws, regulations, and proposed treaties that seek only to cripple our economic might under the false guise of environmental protection.

The simple fact of the matter is that the environmental policies of the past thirty-five years have worked and worked well. Our economy has grown by more than 150 percent since the dawn of the modern environmental era, while the condition of our air, water, and land has improved right along with it. American in-genuity and technological innovation has risen to meet every en-vironmental challenge that has been thrown its way. There is no reason to believe that today's environmental imperatives will frus-trate our ability to meet them. Cleaning up our environment has not robbed our people of prosperity; it has given them, and their children, cleaner air to breathe, purer water to drink, swim, and fish in, and better-protected land to enjoy for generations to come.

We need to recognize, however, that times have changed; we no longer have to rely on the time-wasting process of litigation to produce environmental gains. Rather, we are now poised to make pollution prevention the primary focus of our efforts so that we can protect what we have while cleaning up what has already been damaged. Now is the time to harness the ingenuity of American business, not tie it down by micromanaging its every move. We need tough standards to which every American busi-ness should be held accountable, but we also need to provide op-portunities for companies to reach new goals in ways that keep them economically competitive. Environmental achievements from voluntary efforts must be recognized as real, and credit should be given for early actions.

The continued insistence by many Democrats and much of the environmental lobby for more and more regulation has ham-pered moderate environmental policy making from the left. Yet too many people in the Republican Party continue to act as if the government should have no role in environmental protection because the environment is a losing issue in the polls and Mother Nature will take care of it herself. Early in 2004, the congressional Republican leaders sent out a suggested set of talking points to all House Republican press secretaries for their use in combating accusations that the Republicans have been a disaster for the environment. "Democrats will hit us hard on the environment," the memo predicted. What was the essence of their answer? Deny that there *are* any environmental problems. They actually suggested that Republican members of Congress should use such gems as these to combat criticism of the party's environmental record:

> *Links between air quality and asthma in children remain cloudy and the chance of developing asthma is 3.3 times greater for those children engaging in three sports than for those not playing sports at all* (that's right, if we could just encourage even more kids to become couch potatoes, we could lick the childhood asthma problem).
>
> *Global warming is not a fact* (even though in a 2004 Gallup Poll, 89 percent of the American people believe that global warming will have an effect on the earth's environment).
>
> *EPA data about water pollution in the nation's streams, lakes, and ocean waters is falsely exaggerated* (that's a great argument when nearly eight of ten Americans surveyed named the pollution of America's lakes, rivers, and reservoirs as their greatest environmental concern).

I don't know who the authors of this memo thought they could persuade with such arguments. Fortunately, many moderate House

Republicans, such as Delaware's Mike Castle, were quick to knock down such suggestions. "If I tried to follow these talking points at a town hall meeting with my constituents, I'd be booed," Castle told Gannett News Service.

What's even more disturbing about such suggestions is that they ignore the very real environmental accomplishments of the Bush administration's first term. These included passing the first Brownfields cleanup bill after a decade of trying; committing to an increase in the amount of preserved wetlands in the United States; proposing regulations that would, for the first time, regulate mercury emissions from power plants; requiring a more than 90 percent reduction in soot emissions and a 99 percent cut in sulfur emissions from nonroad diesel engines; providing more than four billion dollars in tax incentives for renewable energy and hybrid and fuel-cell vehicles; nearly doubling funding for climate-change research; more than doubling funding for the Water 2025 initiative to address water quantity and quality challenges.

These accomplishments are noteworthy, but the United States still faces significant environmental challenges. Unless we succeed in shifting the environmental debate away from the extremes and back to the sensible center, we will be unable to meet the challenges we face in a timely and responsible way.

There is no doubt that compromise on the environment is perhaps more difficult today than at any time in the past thirty-five years, and there is plenty of blame to go around. Yet I believe that the party that succeeds in truly presenting a sensible moderate position on the environment—in both word and deed—stands to reap significant policy gains and political rewards. The

Republican Party has the heritage and the record over the past four decades to make it the logical party to do so. What remains unclear is whether it has the vision and the will to move away from the extreme antienvironmentalist posture it has assumed in an effort to solidify its "base."

It's a challenge the moderates must address. To cede the battle for environmental protection to the antiregulatory lobbyists and extreme antigovernment ideologues is to ignore our obligation as stewards of the environment for ourselves, our children and grandchildren. While Hollywood's portrayal of the dangers of failing to address today's environmental challenges may be extreme (as was the case with the film *The Day After Tomorrow*), the issues are real and must be confronted with scientific honesty and moral clarity. Because we share the goal of leaving our air cleaner, our water purer, and our land better protected than we found it, we must also share in advancing the policies that will achieve that goal.

CHAPTER SIX

A Woman in the Party

I will feel equality has arrived when we can elect to office women who are as unqualified as some of the men who are already there.

MAUREEN REAGAN, 1982

President Bush's first administration included more women in high ranking positions than any other in history. When I joined the cabinet, I was one of four women to serve—no president has ever appointed more women to his first cabinet, and only one has appointed as many. President Bush was comfortable with women—and with appointing them to important high-level positions. The president was clearly confident that the American public was ready to see more women in top government positions, and I was gratified that the Republican Party was getting out ahead on that issue. While I never believed the president was driven by a desire to showcase women, I think his efforts to include so many women may have also been part of an effort to speak to the gender gap that has long hobbled Republican politicians of both genders.

Although women are making significant progress in high appointed office, we have a long way to go at every level of government, and Republicans should be concerned. There are almost twice as many women Democrats in Congress as there are Republican women. At the state level, however, the story is different. In 2004, more Republican women (forty-one) held statewide elected office than did Democratic women (thirty-six). What could account for the difference? I believe that when Republican candidates can focus on local issues instead of finding themselves in a referendum on the reputation of the national party, more women are attracted to the GOP and its women candidates are more attractive to the electorate. The success of women candidates at the state level suggests that the party could significantly expand, not only the ranks of Republican women in office at the national level, but also attract many more of the single women voters who have withheld their support from the GOP, if we move away from the harsh rhetoric of wedge issues.

I believe we can make great progress if we try. That's why I was happy to support a group of New Jersey women who established an organization committed to mentoring Republican women who want to get more involved in politics, both behind the scenes and on the ballot. The Christine Todd Whitman Excellence in Public Service Series helps women hone their skills and build a network of contacts. Every year about twenty women from around the state are selected to participate. They meet once a month throughout the year to learn from successful politicians about campaigning and governing. Each participant is also paired with an already accomplished woman in politics or government who provides valuable advice and direction. It encourages them to become more involved in politics and helps them find—and take—their places in the political system.

The Whitman Series does not take positions on issues, nor does it apply a rigid litmus test to those who seek to participate. The women are from varied backgrounds and find themselves at different points in their careers and lives. They hold a variety of opinions on many of the social issues, and yet they share a commitment to the core principles of the Republican Party and understand that despite their differences they can still support one another. As a result, the stage is set for a lively exchange of ideas throughout each session year and across the alumnae network. I find that inspiring, and I wish the party as a whole would follow suit. While women can be as deeply divided and passionate on issues as men, we tend to be less dogmatic in our approach (although there are some notable exceptions on both sides of the aisle). In searching for workable solutions, having more women in decision-making positions can help temper the rhetoric and advance the search for practical answer.

As New Jersey's first woman governor, I was often reminded of just how rare women in high public office still are in our country when people would ask me, "What's it like to be a woman governor—how is it different?" and I always responded, "I don't know. I've never been a male governor, so I have no basis for comparison." Since my gender isn't something I can do anything about, I have tried to avoid letting it define who I am as a political figure, but the difference is obvious. How that difference has actually affected my career is harder to pin down.

I was lucky. I grew up with strong female role models in my mother and my grandmother, both of whom carved places for themselves in politics separate from their husbands. My mother was the Republican national committeewoman from New Jersey for ten years before my father became New Jersey's state chairman, and my grandmother was the head of the New Jersey Federation of Republican Women before my mother assumed the same position. New Jersey was also the home to Congresswomen Florence Dwyer and Millicent Fenwick, both of whom left a mark on an impressionable, budding politician.

All of these role models were real inspirations to me. A woman (especially one who also takes pride in being a wife and mother) who hopes to pursue a successful political career requires more than inspiration, however; she requires support from her family, and I have had that in abundance. What has made my career in politics possible was my good fortune in having a strong partner with whom to share the demands of political life, my husband, John. While politics provided a good fit for me as I was able to balance the demands of young children with part-time political office holding, having the support of my spouse was key. Had John not been there to attend school functions I had to miss or to drive the kids to various events when I couldn't, none of it would have worked. He not only filled the gaps my career created (while still very successfully pursuing his own career), but he was also my chief cheerleader and supporter, urging me on even when I was ready to call it quits.

In many ways our children had a better relationship with their father at an early age than I did with mine. John has been integral to their lives from the beginning. My own father, while always important in my life, commuted every day to New York City during the week and enjoyed playing golf with my mother and older brothers on the weekend, so that I didn't see as much of him as I would have liked during the early years of my own childhood.

While John never hesitated to do more than his fair share in raising the kids and running our household, our daughter, Kate, and our son, Taylor, have also exhibited great patience with the demands of my career. All three of them have believed in me and in what I have tried to do and have given me their complete and unconditional love and support. That has been an indispensable ingredient to my success. They always knew—at least I hope they did—that my family always came first. No matter what happens during the course of your career, it's your family that will always be there and that is something I have always tried to remember. Said another way, you may be a former governor, CEO, beautician, or firefighter but you'll always be a mother or father, sister or brother, aunt or uncle. Those titles never change.

One of the earliest lessons I learned as my political career took shape was that there is no such thing as Superwoman. No one can do it all, at least not all at once. If you are a wife or a mother or in any other way responsible for another person in your life, you will inevitably confront those times when you are torn between responsibilities. Many nights I couldn't sleep agonizing over something I hadn't done for the children or for work. Over time, however, I found the right balance for both my family and my career.

I'll never forget the first time I told my colleagues (all men) on the county board of freeholders, my first elected position, that I would have to miss a meeting because my daughter was playing in an important soccer game. There was a fair amount of judgmental throat clearing in the room, but I couldn't help but notice that after I had opened the door, others followed. In the months and years ahead, some of my male colleagues who had children at home would miss an occasional meeting to attend one of their children's special events. I like to think I helped show my colleagues it was possible to put our kids first and still do our jobs well.

During the course of my political career, I've been reminded of that old description of Ginger Rogers: She did everything on the dance floor that Fred Astaire did, but she did it backward and in heels. There's no doubt that being a woman—and a moderate, Republican woman, at that—has certainly made a difference in how my political career has unfolded. It's hard for many of today's women to recognize how much has changed for women in a relatively short time. When my mother was born, women didn't even have the right to vote. It wasn't until 1933 that the first woman was appointed to a president's cabinet, when Frances Perkins became secretary of labor. Another generation passed before the second woman cabinet member was appointed, and it took yet another generation for the third to be appointed. The United States has yet to join countries such as Great Britain, Pakistan, Israel, and India in electing its first woman head of government.

The challenges women face, from balancing family and career to subtle but still very real discrimination from many men (especially those who constitute the old boys' network), add an additional layer of challenges to an already demanding career. Women in business certainly face those same challenges, but there's another one they don't face—the electorate. In my experience, voters still hold women candidates to a different, and in some ways, more rigorous standard than they do their male counterparts, and women voters are tougher on women politicians than they are on most men. These reasons may be why far too few women serve in public office at the state and national level.

There is no doubt that women are underrepresented in political office in America today. Women make up more than half the population of the United States, yet America's executive mansions, legislative chambers, and city halls see far too few women in positions of power. In 2004, fewer than one in seven members of Congress were women (women Democrats outnumber Republican women almost two to one), and not even one in five governors were women. The 2004 elections didn't do much to improve the picture—the new Congress will see a net gain of five women in the House and no new women in the Senate. Nationwide, fewer than one in four legislative seats are held by women, and of America's ten largest cities, only one—Dallas—has a woman mayor. Women have not moved as rapidly into high-level positions in politics as they have in the corporate sector. From 1995 to 2003, for example, the percentage of women holding corporate officer positions in Fortune 500 companies grew by more than 80 percent. During that same period, the percentage of women serving in Congress grew by less than 40 percent—not even half as fast as in corporate America.

During the seven years I was governor, there were actually times when I was the only woman governor in the country. At least at meetings of the National Governors Association, I didn't have to wait in line for the restroom. Once, while leaving a first ladies lunch at the White House, my husband John joked to Helen Thomas, the dean of the White House press corps, that the event was very poorly planned—forty-nine women and only one John! But when the spouses' group picked breast cancer awareness as its issue, John didn't joke around. He became an avid spokesman, reaching out to men especially, explaining that breast cancer is a family issue and a disease we all have to fight.

One respected national expert, Ingrid Reed, of the Eagleton Institute of Politics at Rutgers University, cites several possible reasons so few women hold elected office: incumbency is strong, and most incumbents are men; the nastiness and negativity of campaigns have discouraged women (and many men) from running; raising money is difficult, though she notes that women candidates who do get the opportunity to run are successful in raising campaign funds. She also writes that—and I can confirm this through my own experience—"Women report that without women in leadership roles, the old boys' network will continue to favor those with whom they are familiar and in many cases have groomed." As in the case of my inaugural parade committee failing to choose bands from minority communities, it's a matter of people (men, mainly, in this case) encouraging and selecting people they know and with whom they are comfortable working.

Yet, even with this discouraging record, New Jersey is one of only twenty-one states that have ever had a woman governor. Why was I able to win in New Jersey? In an odd way, it happened not in spite of the system, but because of it. The roots of my governorship were planted during my 1990 run for the United States Senate against the popular two-term incumbent senator Bill Bradley. No one wanted to take on the former basketball star and Rhodes scholar. Male candidates with serious statewide ambitions took a pass on the race. As the *New York Times* reported that spring, "One of the least desired pursuits in the Garden State is running against Senator Bill Bradley, the Democrat who many voters hope will be the first New Jerseyan in the White House since Woodrow Wilson."

The long-shot status was fixed in people's minds because the same scenario had played out six years earlier. Even during his first reelection campaign in 1984, Bradley seemed unbeatable, and most Republicans decided to spend that election on the sidelines. The solution in 1984 (and again in 1990) was to appear more inclusive as a party by "allowing" a woman to run for the United States Senate, normally one of the most desired political offices in any state. Sure enough, the result was a landslide by any measure—Bradley beat Republican challenger Mary Mochary by an almost two-to-one margin. Mochary, a smart, capable, talented woman who should have had a bright political future, was never heard from again. Had Bradley looked vulnerable, the party leaders, of course, would have anointed one of the up-and-coming members of their old boys' network to make the race.

In 1990, when Bradley would again be running for reelection (and again seemed unbeatable), I decided to throw my hat in the ring. I had no expectation of winning, but because the political climate in New Jersey was in turmoil, with the state's new Democratic governor already courting deep political opposition by proposing various unpopular tax increases, I thought that if I could run a respectable race against Bradley, I'd get good exposure and experience as a statewide candidate and perhaps set up a future gubernatorial race. Once again, because Bradley seemed such a sure bet, the old boys' network was happy enough for a woman to run, and no one seriously challenged me for the nomination.

Actually, I had a bit of history with the senator. The first time I met Bill Bradley was in 1969. I was a year out of college and working for Donald Rumsfeld in the Office of Economic Opportunity. Bradley, who had already achieved national fame as captain of the 1964 U.S. Olympic basketball team and as a member of the New York Knicks, decided he wanted to spend the off-season working for the federal government in Washington. His impending arrival as a summer hire was creating quite a buzz among the staff, even if it managed to completely escape the attention of the press (can you imagine what a field day the media would have today if a sports superstar decided to spend the summer as a glorified summer intern in an obscure government office?). Perhaps because we shared a New Jersey connection, Bradley was initially assigned to work with me. So imagine my surprise when, on his first day in the office, he was introduced to me and then promptly asked me to get him a cup of coffee—no doubt because I was a young woman, and I was there. I quickly explained that he was there to work with me; I was not there to work for him. I also told him where he could get his coffee (and resisted the temptation to tell him what he could do with it).

In 1969, such behavior wasn't unusual; young women in Washington were only just beginning to occupy jobs that didn't involve getting coffee for the men in the office. Many of the men had no idea how to interact with us—especially when we were in rooms that had long been the exclusive domain of men. I remember being in one policy meeting that Rumsfeld was chairing when one of the men swore. One of my colleagues, an older man, immediately stepped forward to defend my honor: "Don't use that language," he berated my foul-mouthed colleague, "there's a lady present!" Rumsfeld quickly stepped in to calm the waters, "Oh, don't worry about Christie; she's just one of the guys." Well, I was thrilled—I thought I'd really arrived.

Bradley and I met again twenty-one years later in that Senate race, and although he never asked me to get him coffee when we met in our two debates, his condescending attitude suggested he still saw me in that light. It was a perspective many political pundits also held. A *Los Angeles Times* article from June 17, 1990, was headlined, SEN. BRADLEY'S RACE IN NEW JERSEY LOOKS LIKE ANOTHER EASY SLAM-DUNK. I wasn't even mentioned until the end of a rather long article. Right after the primary, the Associated Press reported that former governor Tom Kean, in whose second-term cabinet I had recently served, said that although he supported me, he thought Bradley was "unbeatable." That assessment was unchanged throughout the campaign. I had difficulty raising money because no one wants to contribute to a hopeless cause. We tried to get President Bush (an old family friend—my mother had chaired his New Jersey finance committee when he ran for president in 1980) to campaign for me; the White House refused—they wanted him to spend his time campaigning for candidates they believed had a chance. They wouldn't even grant me a brief photo op when the president made a short stopover at Newark airport.

The National Republican Senatorial Committee, which had pledged two hundred thousand dollars to pay for TV and radio ads in the closing days of the campaign, lost hope and reneged on their pledge, sending that money to other candidates around the country who they felt had a better chance of winning. As a result, we had no money to run campaign ads for the last ten days of the campaign. By Election Day, Bradley would outspend me by a twelve-to-one margin—he spent more than twelve million dollars—whereas my campaign was able to raise and spend just under a million. Two days before the election, the *New York Times* wrote that, "none but the most optimistic supporters give her any realistic chance of defeating Mr. Bradley. . . ."

Despite the lack of serious attention from the media and the party, I felt as if the traditional Republican message I espoused—lower taxes and less government interference in people's lives—was resonating with a voting public that had been hit by the biggest state tax hike in history by a Democratic governor. This was compounded by Bradley's refusal to take a position on those tax hikes. He didn't support them; he didn't oppose them. He just avoided the issue altogether. That aloof distance from the most important issue on voters' minds did not help him connect with the electorate, nor did it inoculate him from the backlash that was building. The hundreds of hours I had spent on the campaign trail meeting thousands of voters from all over the state made me think we were making headway, even if no one else thought so.

During the campaign, when my daughter, Kate, then thirteen, and son, Taylor, eleven, were concerned that we might have to move to Washington, I assured them that that was the last thing they should worry about. I felt confident that we wouldn't suffer a disastrous defeat, but I had no real expectation of winning. Although I would have been proud to serve in the Senate, I saw this campaign as a chance to broaden my political contacts and increase my visibility to voters.

After the polls closed, my extended family and I were together in a room in the hotel where my supporters had gathered. When the early returns started coming in, to everyone's surprise, they showed me ahead. As more totals were reported, and we were still ahead, the excitement really started to build—it looked like we just might pull off the political upset of the year. But not everyone shared in the growing jubilant expectation of victory. As the latest batch of returns came in—still showing me ahead—my son became very upset and said, "Mom, you promised we wouldn't have to move to Washington!"

As it turns out, we didn't. I ended up losing the race by just under three points, and by the time I made it to Washington, to join President Bush's cabinet in 2001, my son was finishing college. But that night, even after it became clear that I would not win, my mother, who knew the state well and who had taught me as much about politics as anyone else, didn't want me to concede. I told her, "Ma, we're behind by fifty thousand votes, and the precincts that still haven't reported don't have enough votes in them to make up that sort of deficit." But she wouldn't hear it—she wanted to wait until every last vote had been counted (and recounted, if necessary).

As much as I wanted to honor her request, I placed the call to Senator Bradley and conceded the race. I then went down to the hotel ballroom, where the ranks of my loyal supporters had been swelled by politicians from all over the state, many of whom just hours earlier wouldn't have been seen with me on the campaign trail. I felt great; we had far exceeded everyone's expectations (with the possible exception of my mother's), and I was already looking to the governor's race three years away. My mother passed away just a few months later, never knowing that election night in 1990 wasn't the end of my political career, but really the beginning. How much I wish she had been there three years later. She really would have loved it!

Two days after the election, *Roll Call* (the Washington-based "Newspaper of Capitol Hill") concluded that "Republicans must be kicking themselves for not pouring more time and money into Whitman's effort. Whitman, 44, was not considered a potential upset possibility, but she kept Bradley, 47, and Democrats on the edge of their seats until late Tuesday night." What *Roll Call* didn't report, but which I later discovered, was that none of the candidates to whom the National Republican Senatorial Campaign Committee had diverted the money they pledged to me had won. In fact, none of them came as close to winning as I did.

The real winner that night, though, was my family. Had I been elected, the demands of the Senate would have put an even greater strain on my husband, John, and our two children. As I would learn years later during my tenure at the EPA, I did not like splitting my time between home and Washington. As I said at the time I left EPA, my husband and I had been married for more than twenty-seven years, and we found we liked living together more than we liked living apart. I was in Washington or traveling around the country (and sometimes around the world) at least five days a week, and there were too many occasions when I wasn't even able to make it home on weekends. Fortunately, however, seeking the governorship, and then serving as governor, did not pose quite the same challenge. Because New Jersey is a geographically compact state, I was usually able to spend most nights at home, just as I had in the early days of my political career.

Except for the times I was traveling out of state, rare was the time I couldn't be with John at night.

Like any politician, I made my share of gaffes—but there were some that took on a decidedly different flavor because I was a woman. One day I hopped on a swing at an urban playground dedication and promptly fell off backward, landing on the ground with my legs in the air. My tumble was captured in a series of still photographs snapped by one of the news photographers covering the event. It made all the front pages, as it would have had it happened to a male politician. The difference, however, is that I was wearing a skirt. Fortunately, the skirt was long enough that I didn't end up giving a new meaning to the term full disclosure. I also remember the ribbing I received from my staff and state trooper detail when I misspoke at an annual Breast Cancer Awareness Month event, and declared October to be Breast Awareness Month in the state of New Jersey. Of course, a male politician probably wouldn't have gotten off as lightly as I did if he had made a similar gaffe.

As I said before, through most of my public life, despite the challenges, a career in politics has been a good fit for me—it has enabled me to balance the demands of my career with the priorities of my family while allowing me to make a difference. The first elected office I held was on the county governing board. Because it was a part-time position and the board's meetings were held in the evening, I could be home when the kids got home from school, and I was able to attend their daytime assemblies and after-school games.

One of my first assignments on the board came about because no one else wanted it. For ten years the county had been trying to build a new courthouse. The previous board had picked an architect, but not a site, largely because controversy was swirling around the choice of a site and design for the new building. The presiding judge, for example, threatened to sue if he was unhappy with the location, or if his chambers and courtroom weren't to his liking. I felt as if we had made real progress when we were able to reach agreement on both the location and design. But an even bigger challenge lay ahead—getting the courthouse built—on time and on budget, and that meant working with the construction trades.

When I walked into the room to meet for the first time with all the male shop leaders from the trades and unions, I faced a pretty skeptical group of guys. But they quickly got over it when they realized I would be signing their paychecks—and that I knew what I was doing (my father and grandfather had, after all, built Rockefeller Center) and wasn't afraid to insist on getting it done right. In the end, we brought the building in on time and under budget. Even today, every time I drive by that building I feel a sense of satisfaction in the role I played in helping to get it built.

Although it was a real baptism by fire for me, I thought then and still do that politics is a good career for women. A lot of positions are part-time, and the hours are often flexible. You can also go in and out of politics as your life and needs dictate. Still, most women start in elective office and high-ranking appointed offices later than most men. Even in my administration, the women who served as chief of staff were considerably older than the men who served in that position, reflecting the fact that they had spent their earlier years raising families.

Surely there are many impediments to women's jumping into a career in politics. As the primary caregivers both to America's children and aging parents, many women are reluctant to commit themselves to work that has such an unpredictable schedule and unrelenting demands. Many women want to, or must, work outside the home to earn the income to make a better life for themselves and their families. In addition, women candidates have found it difficult to break into the still male-controlled financial networks that manage campaign fund-raising. For those who are able to contend with those issues, one important change has to happen: women need to do a better job supporting other women who decide to enter the political arena.

The need women candidates have for a counterpart to the old boys' network (although I don't think I'd call it the old girls' network) became obvious in 1993, when I sought the Republican nomination for governor. Given my success in 1990—nearly beating the unbeatable Bill Bradley—I was widely seen as having the inside track for the nomination. I had spent the previous two years preparing for the race. I traveled the state, campaigning and raising money for local, county, and state legislative candidates. I wrote a weekly newspaper column, and I began to build a campaign organization. Yet despite the near upset in 1990, the work I had done in the intervening two years, and the strong levels of support I was registering in the polls, I ended up facing a very difficult primary challenge.

Unlike three years earlier, when no one wanted to take on Bill Bradley, this time it looked like the Republicans would be favored to win—and thereby take back the governor's office. Despite all the years I had spent in the party as an active member, I was clearly not a product of the party apparatus, even though my parents had been so active and involved years before. I owed fewer people favors, which meant I was much less likely to find myself beholden to the old boys. When I announced my candidacy in early 1993, I had no expectations that I would cruise to the nomination. According to the *New York Times,* when my two primary opponents jumped into the race, "Mrs. Whitman already had a nearly two-year head start during which she lined up the support of virtually every Republican county leader, many in the party's conservative leadership and the backing of scores of clubs and professional organizations." It was soon clear that many of the leaders who had publicly pledged their support were working behind the scenes for one or another of my opponents.

I am sure there were many reasons why, even though the party had a demonstrated vote-getter ready to make the race (me), the party's leaders didn't try to limit the potential damage that a hard-fought primary campaign could inflict. I am also sure that one of those factors was that many of them were afraid a woman couldn't win, whereas others were afraid I actually would. At the time, I didn't see this as clearly as I probably should have. In retrospect, with the benefit of both hindsight and experience, it's clear that my gender was a factor in the party leadership's decision not to exercise their power to avoid a primary battle.

It was during the primary that the issue of wealth and class were first used against me. I was somewhat bemused the first time one of my primary opponents suggested that my family's money rendered me unable to connect with average voters because I'd "never had to decide between paying the mortgage and paying for food." I found this tactic somewhat curious coming from my opponent, not only because he was a wealthy corporate lawyer, but also because he had served as chief counsel and attorney general under Governor Tom Kean, a direct descendant of the first colonial governor of New Jersey, who grew up with far greater privilege than I had known. Tom Kean most certainly never had to choose between a mortgage payment and a grocery bill. Yet my opponent never questioned Governor Kean's ability to understand the problems and priorities of New Jersey's voters.

When Kean first ran for governor himself, similar questions about his background arose. But he was able to put them to rest with one clever photo op of his drinking beer in a working class bar in Bayonne, New Jersey. In my case, I was never really able to put the class issue entirely behind me. No amount of grocery shopping, driving my kids to their soccer games, or walking my dogs made me a "regular gal," especially to the mostly male press corps. Looking back, I think that was caused by, at least in some measure, deep-seated stereotypes that exist about wealthy women versus wealthy men. A wealthy woman who enters politics, especially when she is married, as I am, to a successful man (John is a founding partner of his own venture capital firm), is more likely to be seen as a superficial and shallow dilettante—one of the "ladies who lunch"—merely seeking a diversion. On the other hand, wealthy men who enter politics (even when they've inherited their money, as Tom Kean, Nelson Rockefeller, and John Kennedy did), are more likely to be seen as fulfilling their obligation to "give something back" in return for all they've been given.

The sexism I confronted, although certainly not overt, was nevertheless present. Studies have shown, for example, that women are more likely to be portrayed as not tough enough to win or unlikely to be able to carry a campaign all the way to victory. That tactic was certainly used against me in the primary, when one of my opponent's main themes was that he was more likely to defeat the incumbent Democrat in the general election, even though polls showed that I was running ahead of the incumbent by a much bigger margin than either of my opponents. Newspapers would frequently report on what I was wearing on the campaign trail as if I were running for the best-dressed list and not public office. One male reporter wrote that I looked "too aristocratic, too serene, in her tweed jacket and gold jewelry, every hair on her head neatly in place" to represent the middle-class voters who were angry at my opponent's tax and economic policies. Another called me Tom Kean in pearls. (As a result, I never again wore pearls at work.) I don't recall ever reading that my opponents were wearing "handsome blue pinstripe suits perfectly coordinated with red silk ties." During the general election, my opponent always referred to me as "Mrs." Whitman, condescendingly drawing out the pronunciation of "Mrs." as if to emphasize that no "Mrs." could ever govern the state of New Jersey. That technique is still favored among my political opponents. The staff of my Democratic successor in Trenton would sometimes refer to me in the press as "Mrs. Whitman" (usually when they were attacking me), even though they always afforded our male predecessors the courtesy title of "governor."

I know to some these may seem like petty slights, but there's no doubt in my mind that they are designed to marginalize women. There are times, of course, when turnabout is fair play. In 1990, when I was running against Bill Bradley, we had a very difficult time getting him to agree to any debates. As an incumbent sitting on what he thought was a huge lead, that was a smart tactic for him to take. I, on the other hand, needed the exposure and the stature a successful debate could provide. So after months of unsuccessful attempts, I decided to play the "sexist" card. My campaign issued a press release that recounted our months of efforts to schedule debates and quoted me as saying, "I can only conclude that Mr. Bradley believes it is beneath him to debate a woman. Or else he is just plain afraid to debate." Within hours, Bradley's campaign agreed to two live debates—debates that helped establish me as a credible alternative in the eyes of the voters.

No matter how hard any woman tries, it's difficult to avoid noticing that every time we step into the political arena, we are in a distinct minority down there on the arena floor, and many men automatically doubt whether we are tough enough and strong enough to do political battle. One paper wrote during the general election, "Voters, including Republicans, grouse that Mrs. Whitman is not tough or aggressive enough—a frequent complaint about women candidates." In fact, during that campaign when we ran what could be considered the only negative ad against my opponent (we suggested he might be the worst governor of New Jersey since William Franklin, New Jersey's final colonial governor who was arrested for maintaining his loyalty to the Crown during the Revolution), our internal campaign polls showed my positive ratings went up, suggesting that voters were pleased to see I was tough enough to take the gloves off.

During that campaign, I also was widely criticized for keeping a promise to my family. Although conventional political wisdom states that nothing happens during the summer on campaigns and that the public doesn't even start to pay attention until after Labor Day, I was castigated for taking one week off to go mountain biking in Idaho with my family, proving that I didn't have the requisite "fire in the belly" to be governor. Well, if you had two teenage kids longing for privacy and the media was following you everywhere, you'd leave the state, too. It had always been important to John and me that we all experience something new together as a family at least once a year. Family vacations were—and remain—sacrosanct.

Over my years in politics, attitudes have changed. During my first campaign, when I was running for Somerset County freeholder in 1982, more people told me they wouldn't vote for me because I was a woman than told me they would vote for me because of my gender. More recently, I think there's been a shift in attitude, although I still believe there are those who wouldn't vote for a woman regardless of her qualifications. Nevertheless, I've found that the there are many benefits in politics to being a woman. My campaign attracted many talented individuals, including women who found for the first time that they were playing a substantial role in what had always been a man's world in New Jersey. Many of my campaign's senior staff were women, and when I became governor I had the opportunity to appoint a number of highly talented women to senior government posts. In addition, Republican women in the legislature and in local and county offices across the state gave me tremendous levels of support. There was a certain energy that accompanied my status as the first woman in my state's history to be elected governor that I had not seen in any of the other campaigns in which I had participated.

When I won, the papers highlighted the fact that I was the first woman elected governor of New Jersey, which was an important milestone. Because of my gender, my election was a national story. What was mentioned less frequently was the fact that I was also the first person to defeat an incumbent governor in the general election in modern New Jersey history. That, frankly, was more satisfying to me than the other first, although having the portrait of a female governor hanging in the state house reminds young girls they can be anything.

As I prepared to take office and announced my appointments to various senior administration positions, I began to hear that I was appointing "so many women" to my cabinet and staff. I appointed the first woman chief of staff and the first woman attorney general, whom I also later appointed the first woman chief justice of the New Jersey Supreme Court. During the course of my administration, every single senior position in the governor's office was, at one time or another, held by a woman. That might explain why we started to hear comments from down the hall (where the legislature resides) about the governor's office becoming an "estrogen palace." I didn't let criticism—even from within my own party—stop me from appointing the best people.

Of course, it's not enough just to hire women. As the chief executive, you have to set the tone. Women-friendly—and for that matter—family-friendly policies made it possible for many women and men to work in my administration and still have a life—a novel idea in politics. Unless something blew up or fell down, I didn't call staff at two o'clock in the morning. The annual beach party—a governor's office tradition—began including spouses and kids. I had many women with young children on my staff serving in senior positions. Many more women—including those in positions of authority like cabinet members and senior governor's office staff—had children during my administration and were able to return to work. I carried that same approach to the EPA, appointing women to such top jobs as deputy administrator, chief of staff, chief of policy, press secretary, and numerous other senior posts. I once observed in a speech to a women's group that at my morning senior staff meetings the women far outnumbered the men, and joked that the men were only there to demonstrate my commitment to equal opportunity. I had to laugh when shortly thereafter, a disgruntled male employee somewhere deep in the EPA bureaucracy asked the agency's Office of Civil Rights to investigate my hiring practices, claiming my speech proved I discriminated against men.

These appointments were not, of course, just for show. Putting women in office is more than a matter of equity. I believe it's important to have more women involved in politics—and serving in elected office—because women bring a different perspective and a different set of life experiences to their jobs than men. Our way of solving problems can differ from our male counterparts as well. We also tend, I think, to set a different tone in how we work together as a team. I've been told by many people who worked for me over the years that they were impressed that in my offices, people worked together much more collegially than they did in offices run by men. There was less competition to see who got the credit when things went right and who got the blame when things went wrong. Instead, they saw a greater sense of teamwork, where people sought to work with one another in pursuit of larger goals, rather than pursue their own personal goals at the expense of others. I always felt that my responsibility was to find the best person for a job, set out the agenda and goals, and let them find creative ways to get there. I was never uncomfortable with the fact that I couldn't know, or do, everything.

While I have never said that government would be perfect if it was run by women exclusively, I am often tempted to say it couldn't be much worse! Women do have something unique to offer to politics in American today. I don't believe that there are any issues that are exclusively of interest to women, but we often prioritize differently. And since we are the primary caregivers in our families, it's important that our voices be heard because they make a difference.

In 1995, during my first term as governor, I learned that new mothers were being discharged from hospitals in as few as twenty-four hours because insurers wouldn't cover longer stays. I pushed for and signed legislation requiring insurers to cover at least a forty-eight-hour hospital stay for women undergoing a routine delivery and ninety-six hours for those having a caesarean section.

A short time before I signed New Jersey's bill, the state of Maryland had enacted legislation requiring a forty-eight-hour stay for all new moms (if ordered by a doctor). Our bill (which became the model for a federal law enacted the following year) went further—New Jersey was the first state to require even longer stays for moms who undergo C-sections and to give all new moms the final say. As I said at the time, "I've had two children—one each way—and I know that 24 hours is not enough." That's a statement no man could ever make.

Although that particular bill was sponsored by male legislators, it was pushed by women legislators, who told me that they felt empowered by having a woman in the governor's office. Having a woman governor down the hall no doubt affected what got on the legislative agenda—and agenda setting is one of the most important aspects of governing. The agenda determines which issues are dealt with and which are ignored. In my first term alone, I signed bills that made AIDS counseling and testing a standard part of obstetrical care, ensured the death penalty or guaranteed life behind bars for anyone who rapes and murders a child, and leveled the playing field for women and minorities in the awarding of government contracts, to name just a few.

Interestingly, as a politician I have found that my relationship to women voters is definitely different from that of a male politician to male voters. When a man wins an election, men don't think, "Great, we've got a man in there now!" Men are used to seeing other men in positions of political power. But a woman in politics, and in other spheres as well, becomes the banner carrier for all women, and in a way bears the burden of success or failure for all women. Because of that, I have enjoyed a much more personal relationship with the women of my state. Many have approached me to say how proud it made them to have a woman governor and how much confidence it gave them. Interestingly, during my first gubernatorial campaign, we found that older women and stay-at-home moms were less supportive of my candidacy than younger women who worked outside the home, but after I was elected, I received positive affirmation from all different kinds of women, especially if they had young daughters. Fathers of daughters also let me know that they thought it was great that their girls had a role model to look up to. One of my staff members even had a young son who thought only women could be governors!

Another definite difference is the number of women's groups to which I spoke as governor. In the first year alone, I attended eighty so-called women's events—political and nonpolitical—in New Jersey and nationally. Considering how much competition there is for time on any governor's schedule, let alone the multiple opportunities there are to address the same type of event, that certainly was a change. I know some of the men on my staff thought I was going to too many women's events. But I recognized that just because I had spoken to one group of women didn't mean I'd spoken to all women and could cross them off my list. Like men, we cannot be pigeonholed into any one category. And, like men, we deserve equal access to and attention from the people running our government.

The morning after my election as governor, one New Jersey newspaper ran a cartoon that showed me—dressed like Wonder Woman—crashing through the top of the statehouse dome. The caption read, WHITMAN BREAKS THE GLASS CEILING. That cartoon has hung in every one my offices since. I have never believed that women have to possess superhuman powers to succeed in politics, but over the years it has become increasingly clear to me that we need to make a superhuman effort, not just for ourselves, but for other capable women who share our principles.

Today, eighty-five years after women were finally granted the right to vote, five states have never sent a woman to Congress, and twenty-nine have never elected a woman governor. Most states have elected only a few women; only three have sent ten or more women to represent them in Congress over the past eighty-five years. It is long past time for women to assume their full and rightful place in American political life.

So what can we do? Although we don't have strength in numbers when it comes to holding office, we should find strength from one another. Two of my female cabinet colleagues—Gale Norton at Interior and Ann Veneman at Agriculture—and I formed a small group Gale dubbed the Resource Chicks because we each had responsibility for some aspect of America's great natural resources.

We would get together every month or so for lunch. Our talk almost always focused on the many overlapping issues we were facing. It was nice to spend time with other women who were facing some of the same pressures I was, even if we did not spend much time talking about them. We also knew we were always there for each other, as well as for Elaine Chao, the secretary of labor, who was another valued colleague. When Ann Veneman was diagnosed with breast cancer and bravely decided to continue to work even through her treatment, Gale and I were among the many women in the administration who made sure she knew she could lean on us if the need arose.

Women in politics have an obligation to support each other

and to bring more women into the arena. I was fortunate; I had my mother and my older sister as role models for women in politics. But very few women have that same good fortune. That is why we must be deliberate about being mentors to qualified women, we must support them in their efforts, we must celebrate their success, we must help pick them up when they stumble, and we must look for opportunities to help them get ahead. That is what I have tried to do—from appointing many "female firsts" to campaigning and raising money for women candidates from Maine to Hawaii.

Mentoring must be an important part of our work, not just one on one but in a systematic way. If women ever hope to reach a critical mass in politics, we must consider quality and quantity. After all, eighty-five years after getting the vote, we're still playing catch up. The Whitman Series is just one of several mentoring programs run by Republicans throughout the country, including the Lugar Series in Indiana, the Lincoln Series in Illinois, and the Anstine Series in Pennsylvania. Both parties also have organizations that support pro-choice women already running for office: the WISH List and EMILY's List, to name just two.

In New Jersey it is enormously encouraging to see so many bright, energetic women from all over the state so enthusiastic about politics. Since the Whitman Series was founded in 1998, just over one hundred women have completed the program. Nearly two thirds of them have since either run for elected office or been appointed to a government or party position. I am proud to see that just six years after its founding, the series is already having such a positive affect on women's participation in politics in New Jersey.

I hope that this effort and other such programs across the country will encourage more and more women to make politics a part of their lives. I strongly believe there is both a place and a need for more women in American politics at every level—from the polling place, to campaigns, to running for local and national office.

Over the past fifty years, women have served as presidents or prime ministers in more than three dozen countries around the world, including in the world's oldest democracy, Great Britain; the world's largest democracy, India; and the world's most embattled democracy, Israel. Yet here in the world's greatest democracy, no woman has even been able to win the nomination of a major party for president. I hope I will see that trend broken in my lifetime. I believe the country is ready; the question is, are the two parties?

CHAPTER SEVEN

A Time for
Radical Moderates

*If you believe that government should be accountable to the people,
not the people to the government . . . if you believe a person should
be treated as an individual, not as a member of an interest group . . .
if you believe your family knows how to spend your money better
than the government does . . . then you are a Republican.*

ARNOLD SCHWARZENEGGER, 2004

What will it take to move the Republican Party back toward
the center? During the 2004 convention, I, along with
Newt Gingrich and others, participated in a panel discussion
sponsored by the Republican Main Street Partnership, an organization of sixty-nine centrist Republican members of Congress and
governors from thirty-one different states in every part of
America, which is "committed to building America's principled
but pragmatic center within the Republican Party and throughout the nation." Not surprisingly (this was after all a group of

moderates), the discussion was measured and polite. You would be hard pressed to find much in the way of bombastic rhetoric, sharply worded attack T-shirts, or conspiracy theory books at a gathering like this. It's not in the nature of centrists to be extreme. As the headline on an article I saw the next day put it, MODERATES OBJECT, QUIETLY, TO THE PARTY'S DRIFT TO THE RIGHT.

That about sums it up. The centrists in the Republican Party (me included) have, for too many years now, failed to assert themselves as strongly as they should have in insisting on their rightful place in the party. As the respected political journal *Congressional Quarterly* put it in 2002, "Republican moderates have endured [this criticism] for years and have sometimes acknowledged [it] themselves: They set their sights too low to make a difference . . . and when they do rebel against their leadership, they are often easily bought off." It's time for Republican centrists to become radical moderates—people ready to fight for what they believe even if it makes some waves in the party. We have, quite frankly, been too willing to go along to get along, and that has weakened our ability to influence the direction of the party.

The term "radical moderate" appears to be an oxymoron. I just entered the word "radical" into my word processor's thesaurus and found synonyms such as "extremist," "diehard," "militant," and "fanatic." By definition, it would be impossible to be a "militant moderate"; that would be even harder than being a "girlie-man." My quick search, however, highlighted another word, "activist," which I think fits. It is time for moderates in the Republican Party to become activists—activists for the sensible center, for reasonable policies based on fundamental Republican principles, which address the challenges America faces at home and in the world.

Moderates also have to stop overthinking every issue, particularly with regard to how they talk about their beliefs. The social fundamentalists have been expert at distilling their ideas into simple language that draws sharp contrasts between "right" and "wrong"—they see very few shades of gray. Moderates, on the other hand, tend to see the nuances in issues. Too often we moderates get trapped by our own thinking, spending so much time considering the many aspects of complex problems that we lead some to think we don't stand for or believe in anything. I am not advocating the oversimplication of policy, but the way in which we communicate our views shouldn't be needlessly complex.

There are those who argue it's hard to motivate moderates, suggesting they aren't as rabid about issues as those at the extremes are. That's true, and I wouldn't want to change it. It's only by creating an atmosphere in which people can work together constructively that things can get done. That doesn't mean there aren't issues and goals that moderates can't get excited and motivated about, things that will both build the party and help restore the sensible center to American political life.

I believe moderates have to pursue a concerted strategy if they want to succeed in returning the party to its traditional, centrist roots. First, they have to decide on the issues that are of most importance—fiscal restraint, reasonable and open discussion of social issues, environmental policies that promote a balanced approach to environmental protection, and a foreign policy that is engaged with the rest of the world. Then they must begin to organize at the local level, involving like-minded moderates in the state and local party structures to ensure that the candidates the party nominates do not represent just the far fringes of the party but instead come from the heart of the party's moderate middle. There's no doubt that moderates have been outorganized, from the precinct level to the national stage, by the social fundamentalists and those who, like them, impose a narrow litmus test on anyone who seeks to carry the Republican banner. The superior ability of the social fundamentalists to turn out their voting base leaves moderate Republicans vulnerable to primary challenges from those who are determined to pick them off one by one. Moderates need to do a much better job of organizing—at every level—so we can help fellow moderates fight off these challenges. As Benjamin Franklin said, "We must all hang together, or assuredly we shall hang separately."

Until moderates are able to build a robust, grassroots, and financial network that can stand up to the firepower of the far right, they will likely and understandably continue to trim their sails, hoping to avoid the sort of expensive, divisive, and ugly primary challenge Senator Arlen Specter had to beat back in 2004. The pieces are already in place. Groups such as the Republican Majority for Choice, the Main Street Coalition, and Republican Leadership Council, to name just a few, are now seeking to energize the moderate base. In 2004, moderates proved yet again their willingness and ability to raise the money necessary to fund campaigns at the national and local level. There are millions of moderate Republicans who can be motivated to support their fellow moderates move the party back toward the center with their time and effort, their money, as well as their votes.

At the national level, moderate Republican leaders must start now to identify and unite behind a highly credible and attractive leader who would be willing to fight for the party's presidential nomination in 2008. They then must begin to work to bring that leader the national exposure that will enable them to mount an effective campaign and build a broad coalition. There's no doubt that the social conservatives, as well as the others in the party who occupy a narrow piece of the political spectrum, have already begun working to identify and advance their potential standard bearers for 2008. Moderates must be every bit as intentional and focused in doing so as well. The time where moderates limit themselves to trying to extract concessions from the candidates advanced by the social conservatives must come to an end. It's time to go for the brass ring.

In addition, elected Republican moderates have to be more willing to use the power of their numbers and their positions to force the party leadership back to the center. In Congress in 2004, for example, 55 of the 229-member House Republican caucus belonged to the Republican Main Street Partnership; in the Senate 9 of the 51 Republicans were members. Without the votes of those moderates, the House and Republican leadership would have a very difficult time passing important legislation. This gives the moderates enormous leverage, even if there could be a short-term price to pay with party leadership. It's time to be radical in the use of what leverage the moderates have.

American politics have become far too polarized, too extreme, too nasty, too unproductive, and still ignored by too many people. The increased turnout in 2004 is a positive development, but even with that rise in voter participation, at least eighty million eligible voters stayed home from the polls. By restoring a sense of purpose, of optimism, of hope, and of vision to our politics, we can repair what's broken. We can make it possible for America to move forward, even in the midst of a dangerous world and real challenges at home, united as a party and as a people behind common goals. Working to heal the breach in American political life is a cause about which people can become excited and that can motivate them to make a difference.

I have talked about the problem the Republican Party has in attracting the votes of African American and other minority voters. Our actions have not always been true to our legacy as the party of Lincoln. I believe, however, that moderates can chart a new course for the party in appealing to and attracting minority voters to our ranks—and that will benefit not just the party but the country as well. Moderate Republicans can take the lead in recruiting black and other minorities, as well as women, to the party, beginning at the grassroots level and working up. It is an embarrassment that in 2004 not a single one of the thirty-nine black members of Congress was a Republican, that just three of the twenty-one Hispanics serving in Congress were Republicans, and that none of the five Asian American members of Congress were Republicans, and only twenty-six of the seventy-seven women in Congress are Republicans. The party showed in 2004 that it can earn increased levels of support from minorities, as it did with Hispanic voters. There's no reason to think that success cannot be built upon.

The Republican Party must do better than that; it must begin recruiting bright, capable, articulate, Republican minority and women candidates at the local level and start grooming them, like it does any other candidate, for higher office. This is an area of party building that has been neglected in the rush to keep the social fundamentalists and their counterparts mollified. Centrist

Republicans can fill the gap that has been left by the current political leadership by taking the lead in building a significant minority presence in the GOP, not because it's "politically correct" but because it's correct politics. Those words I heard from an older black man in Harlem nearly forty years ago during the Listening Tour keep coming back to me: "I think the Republican Party has got an opportunity and doesn't even know it. That is to rebuild, and it is possible if they had the talent around. They could take the blacks away from the Democrats." Moderate Republicans should make this their cause, their mission. If they do, and if they succeed, it will not only help build a new Republican majority; it will also help heal racial and ethnic divisions as both parties have to start competing for the support of minority voters.

Moderate Republicans must also reclaim for the party the issue of fiscal responsibility. We must rededicate ourselves to the proposition stated in the 1960 Republican platform: "Government that is careless with the money of its citizens is careless with their future." The return to deficit spending under a Republican president and Republican Congress is contrary to everything the GOP has always stood for. While much of the increased spending that has contributed to the deficit can be attributed to our national defense and homeland security needs in the wake of September 11, 2001, much of it cannot. As the Cato Institute has pointed out, not since the days of Lyndon Johnson and the launch of the Great Society has nondefense real discretionary spending increased by such large annual margins.

Some have blamed Republican tax cuts for the deficit. I do not agree. Indeed, I am a strong supporter of tax cuts but only when they are accompanied by spending restraint. During my seven years as governor of New Jersey, the Republican legislature and I cut taxes more than fifty times, saving the taxpayers of my state more than eleven billion dollars. At the same time, we held the annual increase in state spending to the lowest levels in a generation, even while increasing funding for local property tax relief, education, and anticrime efforts. When I left office, the last budget I proposed contained a one-billion-dollar surplus.

Of course, I had one weapon the president doesn't have—the line-item veto. If I was presented with a spending bill that contained pork barrel items, I could—and often did—simply eliminate them. That didn't always go over big with the legislator who had managed to insert that special project into the bill, but it sure did make a difference to New Jersey's taxpayers.

Nobody in Washington has done a better job than Senator John McCain in calling attention to the billions of dollars of pork Congress adds each year. The home page of his official Senate Web site prominently features a link to "Latest Pork Statements and Lists." For a good laugh (only it isn't really funny), read his description of some of the pork barrel items included in the 2005 Defense Appropriations Bill. By McCain's accounting, more than two thousand items, totaling nearly $9 billion, were added to the bill, including $3.5 million for sleep deprivation research, $1 million to repair a biathlon trail in Alaska, and $2.8 million for the C-135 Improved Waste Removal System. Because Senator McCain is not shy about pointing out that much of this spending is largely designed to benefit the specific states of some of his colleagues, his efforts aren't very popular on Capitol Hill.

When it comes to seeing spending as pork, the difference is almost always in the eye of the beholder, or whoever's pig is getting gored. Republican moderates should make themselves the true champions of fiscal responsibility and accountability in Congress, both by insisting on spending restraint and by advocating a measure to give the president the constitutional power of the line-item veto. As Ronald Reagan said in 1984, "As governor, I found the line-item veto was a powerful tool against wasteful or extravagant spending. It works in forty-three states. Let's put it to work in Washington for all the people." I'm sure there must be a way to craft a constitutionally sound law to give the president line-item veto authority. We should make it a priority. Until that happens, moderates in Congress should work to tighten the rules to make it harder for legislators to add unrelated special projects to appropriations bills.

The nearly one-hundred-page Republican platform of 2004 contained only ten paragraphs (about one and a half pages) concerning the importance of fiscal discipline, a principle every Republican can agree on, about the same amount of attention devoted to gay marriage and abortion—issues on which the party is not united. The Republican Party should never lose its hold on the issue of fiscal responsibility. Moderates in the party can and should take the lead in reasserting that hold.

Another area where the center of the party must be more vocal and insistent is in the conduct of America's foreign policy. President Bush has earned enormous respect for his response to the terrorist attacks of September 11, 2001. From the creation of the Department of Homeland Security to the strengthening of the capabilities of first responders, he has done much to improve our safety and security at home. Unfortunately, for a wide variety of reasons, America's standing in the world has not improved; to the contrary, it has worsened considerably. I firmly believe that the security of the United States should never be subordinated to the will or whim of any international body or foreign country. However, I also believe that the United States should use that power constructively to build alliances that strengthen our security and that of our allies and advance the cause of peace and freedom in the world.

America is the world's only superpower. With that reality comes responsibility as well as many challenges. While we cannot cede that responsibility to the rest of the world, we can seek assistance from others in the world in bearing it. It is likely that in our lifetime the strength of the economy of the People's Republic of China will rival, if not surpass, our own—and that could very well lead them to political dominance as well. While this eventuality is less certain, Russia also possesses the enormous potential to regain a dominant place on the world stage.

Even today, these nations possess real influence in areas of the world of vital interest to the United States. China, for example, can play a key role in controlling and perhaps even dismantling North Korea's nuclear weapons program. Its interest in a nonnuclear Korean peninsula is at least as compelling as ours. Similarly, Russia must, for reasons of geography if no other, share our concern about a nuclear Iran. In building America's influence in the world, we should be doing more to bring our common interests together into a common cause.

In Russia, that could include making substantial investments in their efforts to reprogram their weapons-grade nuclear materials. It's a program that would not only address a dangerous remnant from the cold war and the days of mutually assured destruction, but would also make the world a safer place by ensuring that such materials do not fall into the hands of terrorists or those states that are seeking to become part of the nuclear club while building goodwill around the world.

For the Chinese, continued support of their efforts to further integrate themselves into the world community through membership in various international organizations and agreements could help strengthen our relationship and could also yield dividends on areas of national security where we share common interests.

Despite the fervent desires of those in the Republican Party who long for the "good old days" of American isolationism, no amount of wishing will change the fact that we are part of a world community. Rather than engaging in a fruitless—and ultimately damaging—effort to withdraw from the world, we should be actively searching for means to engage the world in ways that are consistent with, and advantageous to, our own national interest. The United States has a long history of being able to come through difficulties in the world at large stronger and more influential than before, and Republicans have often been at the forefront of those efforts. There is no reason to believe that cannot continue to be the case.

After all, Republicans have a long legacy of being the most effective and sophisticated practitioners of foreign policy, deftly advancing our own interests while engaging the cooperation of our longstanding allies. From Eisenhower's success in containing the Soviet Union during the early days of the cold war to Nixon's brilliant opening of China and détente with the Soviet Union, to Reagan's determined effort to bring the cold war (and Soviet communism) to an end without firing a single shot, to Bush 41's masterful coalition building in liberating Kuwait in the Gulf War, Republicans have long shown they know how to engage the world to the mutual advantage of our own interests and those of our allies.

Regretfully, that long legacy of mastery of foreign affairs by Republican presidents has not been reflected in more recent years. The war in Iraq, while succeeding in removing Saddam Hussein, has proven to be far more difficult than the president expected or the country was prepared for. It would have been better by far, many believe, if we had focused like a laser on completing the job we had started in Afghanistan before moving on to Iraq.

The White House's efforts to build a strong international coalition in support of the start of the war did not yield the results one would have hoped for and expected. These failures are due in part to the attitude the administration took from its earliest days, as so clearly illustrated by the way in which the United States dismissed the Kyoto Protocol on global warming, as well as other issues of concern to the international community. Our failure to even acknowledge (let alone accommodate) the interests and concerns of other nations when charting our own course has carried a significant cost—a cost that is being measured in American lives, resources, and prestige.

When looking at the difficulties we still face in combating the insurgency in Iraq, these words, spoken by one of the giants of modern world affairs, resonate. "We have, therefore, great difficulties in conducting squalid warfare with terrorists. . . . What is going on now is doing us a great deal of harm in every way and in our reputation all over the world. . . . This is a conflict with terrorists, and no country in the world is less fit for a conflict with terrorists than [ours]. That is not because of weakness or cowardice; it is because of restraint and virtue, and the way of life which we have lived so long."

As current as they sound, these words were spoken in the first half of the twentieth century by Winston Churchill, referring to the difficulties Britain was having in Palestine. On the day he delivered the speech in which those words were contained, the British high commissioner in Palestine ordered the evacuation of the two thousand British civilians living there because their safety could not be guaranteed. Several months later, Britain turned over its responsibility for the area to the United Nations.

Churchill's words could just as easily apply today. The U.S. effort to establish a free and democratic state in Iraq is being met by the same sort of terror tactics that eventually drove Britain out of Palestine. Republican moderates, including Secretary of State Colin Powell, whose advice, I believe, was largely ignored in the runup to the war in Iraq, have an opportunity to help restore Republican foreign policy to the thoughtful, sophisticated, effective level at which it has long been conducted when our party was in the White House. By advocating a renewed effort to build an international coalition of our major allies to bring Iraq into the family of nations, Republican centrists can help President Bush achieve the success in Iraq he so clearly wants, which the Iraqi people deserve, and that the world so clearly needs.

At every level the campaign of 2004 also gave Republican moderates another cause around which to rally—the conduct of campaigns. Campaigns for political office, at all levels, have become increasingly nasty and offensive over the past several decades. Yet it doesn't have to be this way. Political operatives defend the conduct of today's negative campaigning because they say it works, and, to a point, they're right. While politics in America has always resembled an extreme sport (back in 1864, *Harper's* published a list of terms used by Lincoln's opponents to describe him in that election year. "Filthy Story-Teller, Despot, Liar, Thief, Braggart, Buffoon, Usurper, Monster, Ignoramus Abe, Old Scoundrel, Perjurer, Robber, Swindler, Tyrant, Fiend, Butcher"), it's only in the modern age that political attack ads have been brought right into our living rooms.

A variety of polls taken in recent years reveal that strong majorities of American voters dislike negative campaigns. One national poll taken several years ago revealed that almost three-quarters of voters would be more likely to vote for a candidate who agreed to follow a campaign code of conduct. Championing clean campaigns is another area where as a group moderate Republicans could both build their influence in the party and improve voter attitudes toward politics. Temperamentally, they are well suited to the task.

I have some experience on both sides of this issue. In my first race for governor in 1993, my opponent ran a high___ ative campaign against me. During the summer of 2004, I w___ ι tel-evision show with noted democratic strategist Paul B___ vho, along with James Carville, had run my opponent's ca___ ι in 1993. Before we went on the air, Begala was reflecting ___ ef-fort. "We threw everything at you," he recalled, "in ar___ to make you so unattractive no one would want to vote f___ " I remembered it well; among the charges leveled at me w___ ωαt I wanted to let drunk drivers get off easy and that I supported widespread ownership of assault weapons. I used to joke that if all you knew about me was what you'd learned from my opponent's attack ads, you'd think I spent all my time driving drunk and hanging out the car window randomly firing an Uzi.

In the recent annals of New Jersey politics, however, that campaign was just the opening act. The state's 1996 U.S. Senate campaign garnered national attention for the depths to which it sank. With my own reelection scheduled for the following year, I was determined to change things for the better. So on the day after the Senate election, I issued a pledge to clean up campaigning in New Jersey. I said I would run an issues-oriented campaign in 1997 and challenged anyone else who ran to commit to the same thing.

I asked the Eagleton Institute of Politics at Rutgers to host a forum to bring together both state and national political experts to explore how we could accomplish that goal. As a result, guidelines and structures emerged. Probably the most significant was the formation of something called the Issues Index. The index identified the five issues of greatest concern to New Jersey voters and then evaluated all campaign advertisements against that list. Every other week during the campaign, the Issues Index published a report that assessed the extent to which our ads stuck to the issues and provided verifiable claims. It also judged whether the messages were advocating on behalf of a candidate, comparing the positions of each candidate, or just attacking the candidate's opponent. Both my Democratic opponent and I agreed to participate in this process. As the campaign unfolded, we each submitted our campaign ads to the Issues Index for evaluation. Our pledge to keep our campaigns focused on issues and the independent appraisals that were made to hold us to our pledge truly elevated the tenor and tone of that campaign—and the people of New Jersey noticed. Three weeks before the 1997 election, one statewide poll showed that 54 percent of the voters felt the campaign had been positive. That's compared with just 17 percent who had held a similar view the year before. After the election, another poll found that fully 70 percent of voters felt the tone of the 1997 campaign was more positive than in 1996.

As Americans grow increasingly weary of negative campaigning, moderate Republicans can help lead the way to more positive, issues-oriented campaigns at every level of government. This is the sort of good policy that also makes for good politics and that could provide the added benefit of actually improving the reputation of politicians and of the political process. Some will see this as overly idealistic, but I know it can work because I've seen it work.

The election results of November 2004 will be analyzed for years. What's important to our politics, however, is how the party responds to those results in the near term. President Bush's victory has led many to conclude that the best way for the Republicans to win is by targeting the base. We must be careful, however, to avoid taking away lessons that may not really be there. It could just as easily be true that the president's win was only the latest in a long line of victories by incumbent commanders in chief during times of war. After all, no American president has ever been denied reelection during wartime.

So before the Republican Party institutionalizes the politics of making the red states redder and ignoring the rest of the country, it must decide whether it believes that true political leadership is best advanced by further dividing the nation in pursuit of electoral victories. I believe pursuing such a course would be a profound mistake. It would not only present a very real danger to the party's continued ability to win elections; it would also call into question whether the party is in fact worthy of governing the United States of America.

The responsibility of ensuring that the party follows the right path lies with those moderates who are willing to work to make it happen. To find out more information about groups that support moderate Republicans and want to move American politics back toward the center visit www.mypartytoo.com. As my father told me more than fifty years ago, "If you don't participate, you lose the right to complain."

ACKNOWLEDGMENTS

Over the past year, I've learned that writing a book is a lot like running for or serving in office—it takes a lot of talented and dedicated people to help you get the job done. Without the help of the people named below, this book would never have been possible.

For the past ten years, Bob Bostock has helped me find the right words in countless speeches, articles, and op-eds. Without his belief that I had a story to tell and something worthwhile to add to the debate, I would have never undertaken this effort. Without his writing skills, research capabilities, and dedication to the project there would be no book. I have been lucky to have him as a partner in this effort and any success it may enjoy will be largely his.

To help jog my memory and bring issues into clearer focus, Eileen McGinnis, my former EPA chief of staff and the head of my office of policy and planning in Trenton, arranged (in her usual thorough and efficient way) an enormously helpful series of roundtable meetings with people who participated at my side through various major events over the course of my career. Eileen also read the manuscript at numerous stages during its preparation, always offering penetrating and useful observations.

Acknowledgments

Nancy Rohrbach, my closest friend for more than thirty years (we got our start together at the RNC with the Listening Program), and Susan Spencer Mulvaney, who headed New Jersey's Washington office when I was governor and served as my deputy chief of staff at EPA, both carefully reviewed the manuscript several times, providing keen political insights and the candid suggestions every author must both dread and earnestly desire to receive.

Carol Cronheim, who joined my gubernatorial campaign in 1993 as a young staffer and went on to serve in several key posts during my years in Trenton, was particularly helpful in shaping the chapter "A Woman in the Party."

All of those who participated in our roundtables and/or read certain parts of the manuscript along the way deserve a special word of thanks for taking the time out of their very busy schedules to remember some good and some not-so-good times and provide important perspective on events. They are: Hazel Gluck, John Farmer, Liz Ferry, Sarah Flowers, Jessica Furey, Tom Gibson, Jane Kenny, Ed Krenik, Pete McDonough, Tucker McNeil, Liz Murray, Judy Shaw, Buster Soaries, Herb Tate, Mike Torpey, Peter Verniero, and Tom Wilson.

Making sure there was always time to do the necessary work is no easy task and I am sincerely grateful to Holly Rogers for handling my schedule on top of everything else.

The people at Penguin Press could not have been more helpful in shepherding this first-time author through what appeared to me, at times, to be an impossible task.

Ann Godoff showed real courage in agreeing to publish a political book whose author made clear, within a minute of the start of their first meeting, that she would not be writing a "tell-all." Her confidence in what I wanted to do was a real inspiration.

My editor, Emily Loose, improved the book with every idea she offered, from the simplest suggestion about the structure of a sentence to broad observations that helped give clearer shape and direction to the book. She is a professional in the truest sense of the word and a real pleasure to work with.

Managing editorial and production performed amazing feats of juggling to enable me to account for the results of the 2004 presidential election in this book while still keeping everything on schedule.

Copy editor Susan Johnson did a meticulous job on the manuscript; where was she when I was writing papers for some of the more exacting English teachers and professors I had in school?

My agent, the irrepressible Gail Ross, believed in this project from the start and used her considerable range of skills to help bring this from a concept in my head to the book you are holding in your hands.

Over the course of my political career, literally hundreds of people have contributed to my success in more ways than anyone can know and more than anyone else can appreciate. Filling a wide variety of roles with real talent and dedication, they gave selflessly of themselves in service to their government and their fellow citizens. I wish I had the space to name them all; they know who they are— I only hope they also know how privileged I feel to have had the opportunity to work with them and how grateful I am to have merited their support.

Just as it's true in public life, it's true with this book: I couldn't have done it without all the help I've received, but whatever shortcomings this book contains are mine and mine alone.

Christine Todd Whitman served in the Bush cabinet as head of the Environmental Protection Agency from 2001 until May of 2003. Prior to that she served as the fiftieth governor of New Jersey—from 1994 to 2001. She lives in Oldwick, New Jersey.